Having read Dee Dee's book *Good to the Last Drop*, I was honored to be asked to review her latest writing, *A Pleasing Aroma*. This book is one that will cause the reader to really look at their life and compare it to God's Word.

Dee Dee doesn't soft soap or pull any punches in this work. Her up-front honesty, even when it involves her own life or that of her immediate family, lets you know every word is from the heart. Thoughts and feelings about dealing with difficult people, the harm we can do with words, bad things happening to good people, God's involvement when we sin, our last day on earth, and the beauty of salvation are just a few of the short discussions Dee Dee has with her readers.

Reading this book for review was very difficult, as it is not one you just sit down and read from cover to cover. It is a daily dose of truth you can chew on and ask yourself if the situation fits the person you see in the mirror. You can see the hand of God in these inspirational stories and when it's food for thought from the Father, you can be sure it will satisfy. I can highly recommend this book and hope it blesses you as much as it did me.

—*Ann Correll, speaker and author of Juvenile Fiction*

A Pleasing Aroma by author Dee Dee Wike is a refreshing book that works well in devotion time each day. The chapters are illustrations of "where the rubber meets the road" in all of our lives. It is not a pretentious work. She does not set herself up as a perfect example in the "how to" of Christianity. She does illustrate the presence of the Lord in everyday situations in which we are all familiar. I identified with most of the topics and really admired her treatment of things like the complications of raising teens, discouragement, joyfulness of life, and all the bumps in the road between the great times we encounter. This book, as well as her last work, is well worth reading.

—*Elaine Littau, author of Christian Historical/Western Fiction*

Dee Dee has successfully bridged the gap between God's Word and everyday life with her examples of the challenges we all are facing, have faced, or will likely face in the future. With every challenge Dee Dee has faced, God has encouraged her with the promises from his Word, giving her hope and power in the midst of everything from tending a pet guinea pig to balancing personal finances.

When I nestled in the lap of my grandmother for my daily devotional she always smelled of fresh roses due to the scented soaps and body powders she used. I know her prayers were fragrant to the Lord, for they sure were to me. As I read Dee Dee's lessons, I offered up sweet fragrant prayers that each of you will be as blessed and encouraged as I am to follow her example of applying God's Word to the most simple or complex situation you are faced with from day to day.

—*Dot Lester, retired*

This book is perfect for busy believers. The devotionals are short, packed full of everyday situations and easy to read. Dee Dee gives the reader hope by giving incidences from her own life, letting them know they are not alone in this walk we call life. I highly recommend this devotional to anyone and everyone.

—Michelle Jinnette, stay-at-home mom and book review blogger

Taking a moment to read any of Dee Dee Wike's inspirational nuggets of wisdom in *A Pleasing Aroma* never fails to cheer a flagging spirit.

In her second nonfiction book, she weaves biblical verse throughout her personal stories of challenge—stories applicable to all of us navigating today's fast-paced life. Just as in her first book, *Good to the Last Drop: Refreshing Inspiration for Homeschool Moms and Other Busy Women*, Wike relates God's promises and messages of hope, love, understanding, and encouragement to everyday living.

These messages offer the polish to buff a drooping outlook into a sparkling reflection of our Maker's image. They surround the reader with strong armor while strengthening the foundation to spread encouragement to others.

—Joan Crowe, former editor and publisher of several weekly newspapers serving suburban towns and cities in the Memphis, Tenn., area.

Dee Dee's devotions are always inspiring as she shares with the readers of *Common Ground Herald* each month, and *A Pleasing Aroma* is no exception. Not only do I find inspiration in these devotions, but I find a challenge to a status quo attitude. I particularly like how at times she includes an evangelistic challenge with many of the practical life applications.

—Tony Kilgore, Publisher and Editor of
Common Ground Herald a regional Christian
Newspaper, CommonGroundHerald.com

A PLEASING
AROMA

A PLEASING
AROMA

Dee Dee Wike

TATE PUBLISHING
AND ENTERPRISES, LLC

This book is designed to provide accurate and authoritative information with regard to the subject matter covered. This information is given with the understanding that neither the author nor Tate Publishing, LLC is engaged in rendering legal, professional advice. Since the details of your situation are fact dependent, you should additionally seek the services of a competent professional.

The opinions expressed by the author are not necessarily those of Tate Publishing, LLC.

Published by Tate Publishing & Enterprises, LLC
127 E. Trade Center Terrace | Mustang, Oklahoma 73064 USA
1.888.361.9473 | www.tatepublishing.com

Tate Publishing is committed to excellence in the publishing industry. The company reflects the philosophy established by the founders, based on Psalm 68:11,
"The Lord gave the word and great was the company of those who published it."

Book design copyright © 2011 by Tate Publishing, LLC. All rights reserved.
Cover design by Kellie Vincent
Interior design by Christina Hicks

Published in the United States of America

ISBN: 978-1-61346-867-8
1. Religion / Christian Life / Inspirational
2. Religion / Christian Life / Devotional
11.09.09

DEDICATION

It is with deep affection and gratitude that I dedicate this book to my family, my friends, and my heavenly Father, who made this project possible through your prayers, encouragement, and financial provision.

Each of you has played a significant role in the completion of *A Pleasing Aroma* by sharing your love and your lives with me. You have taught me much about faith as you have walked beside me in my trials, shouldered my burdens, and prayed me through some difficult challenges during the writing of this book. I love you more than you know.

To the readers of my first book, *Good to the Last Drop*, and my devotional blogs, I send a very special thank you. Not only did you buy the book for yourself, but you gave it to others who needed the encouragement of God's Word. May God bless you richly for the role you have played in this ministry and the lives you have touched simply by sharing this book with others.

FOREWORD

It is a great privilege to write an endorsement for Dee Dee Wike and her book, A Pleasing Aroma. As I read through her second work, it dawned on me that Dee Dee penned her thoughts specifically for me. She could change the title to Devotions for Busy Pastors. I enthusiastically recommend this book, as it nails the heart of the matter for twenty-first century followers of Christ. We are too busy. As she says in the preface, "There just aren't enough hours in the day to do everything life demands of us. Between holding down a job, nurturing important relationships, serving in our churches, and managing a busy household, we often neglect the most important thing of all, our relationship with the Lord." Those are such true thoughts that resonate deeply in my spirit both as a pastor as well as someone bombarded by the tyranny of the urgent.

I recommend this book because it is written from the perspective of someone fully immersed in the reality of life and also from the heart of someone who desperately wants more of the Lord. These bite-sized inspirational thoughts will challenge you, make you laugh, cause you to think, and ultimately encourage you as you pursue more of the Lord. In an early chapter entitled "Falling to Pieces, Finding our Peace," she poignantly comments that "peace does not come from within us or as a result of anything we do. It comes from realizing that God is our daily source of peace." This is an example of the seasoned wisdom that Dee Dee brings to the totality of life responsibilities that each of us face.

If you are under the grind and feeling the tension of not enough hours for everything, then Dee Dee has just the remedy for you. If you are thinking of throwing in the towel and giving up following Jesus because he is just not practical, then give Dee Dee a chance to show you that your faith is perfectly suited for the life God has for you. Be encouraged, be thankful, and most of all, live victoriously!

—*Dr. Ernie H. Frey, Senior Pastor*
Central Church, Collierville, TN

PREFACE

Let's face it—there just aren't enough hours in the day to do everything life demands of us. Between holding down a job, nurturing important relationships, serving in our churches, and managing a busy household, we often neglect the most important thing of all: our relationship with the Lord.

A Pleasing Aroma: Inspiring Devotions for Joyful Living is written for men and women who desire a deeper relationship with God and need the encouragement of his Word but don't have time for in-depth Bible study. Think of it as a spiritual vitamin to supplement your pastor's sermon and keep your faith walk in good shape during the week. It is my prayer that these short devotionals will whet your appetite for a regular intake of God's Word as you see how relevant Scripture truly is for the challenges of daily living.

Because these devotionals are undated and written in an easy-to-read format, you can read as few or as many selections as your schedule allows. If you have to lay aside the book for a day or two, you can easily pick up where you left off or read the selections in random order.

Make the most of your down time by keeping a copy in your car to read while you're in the waiting room or car-pool line. When you have finished the book, please pass it on to another busy believer who needs the encouragement of God's Word.

THE NEXT STEP

Whether you turn to the right or to the left, your ears will hear a voice behind you saying, "This is the way; walk in it."

Isaiah 30:21

We go through many seasons in life, some that are pleasant and others that are not. As we endure times of testing, we pray that God will hold true to his promise to work all things together for our good (Romans 8:28). Although we may not understand exactly what God is up to, we can trust that he has our best interest at heart and that one day we will be able to look back and see how each particular season was masterfully woven into his overall plan for our lives.

As you embark upon a new season in life, one of promise and yet uncertainty, you can trust that God will use all your past experiences to prepare you for whatever lies ahead. Every heartache you have known, sin you have committed, and victory you have won will factor somehow into what he has planned for you. Perhaps even now you can see how God has orchestrated every aspect of your life, weaving his tapestry one stitch at a time.

God's directions are not always neat and specific. Sometimes he simply calls us to trust him as we take the next step. Where are you on your journey in life? Are you willing to take the next step like Abraham, who set out for the Promised Land even though he did not know where God would lead him?

The grandest adventure of our lives takes place when we surrender everything to God and take that next step, trusting in him to direct or, if necessary, redirect us. Dare to believe in God and everything he has promised in his Word. Step out in faith, believing that God knows the way even if you don't.

IT COULD HAPPEN TOMORROW

The sun will be turned to darkness and the moon
to blood before the coming of the great and
glorious day of the Lord. And everyone who calls
on the name of the Lord will be saved.

Acts 2:20–21

The Weather Channel's *It Could Happen Tomorrow* is a
television program that depicts what could happen if a
certain natural or weather-related disaster occurred. Using
history, science, and computer models, it predicts future
conditions based on past or current events and scientific
data. When I watch this program, I am often keenly aware
that I am unprepared for any sort of natural disaster.

While we may never be prepared for a catastrophic natural disaster, there is one world-changing event we can plan for—Christ's return. The Bible tells us that Jesus Christ is coming again and that in the days before his return, we "will hear of wars and rumors of wars...nation will rise against nation, and kingdom against kingdom. There will be famines and earthquakes in various places" (Matthew 24:6-7). In recent years haven't we seen an escalation of natural disasters, war, and famine throughout the world? Are you prepared for the day when you will be called from this earth in the twinkling of an eye to live with him in heaven?

If you are not prepared, then today is the day you need to make a life-saving decision—one that will preserve you for all eternity. No matter what happens in this life, we each must be born again of the Spirit through salvation in Jesus Christ if we are to live eternally in heaven. That is the simple truth. All the bottled water, food staples, and Duracell batteries in the world won't save you. Only Christ can. Receive him as Savior today and settle the question of your eternal security once and for all.

FALLING TO PIECES, FINDING OUR PEACE

You will keep in perfect peace him whose mind is steadfast, because he trusts in you. Trust in the LORD forever, for the LORD, the LORD, is the Rock eternal.

Isaiah 26:3–4

For some, life doesn't seem to let up. While there are those whose lives are relatively peaceful with manageable trials of short duration, there are others who seem to live in the valley of despair with little hope of finding the peace that continually eludes them. All of us are in one place or the other. What is it that differentiates the ones who have found peace from those who cannot seem to attain it no matter what they do? Therein lies the answer—peace does not come from within us or as a result of anything *we* do. It comes from realizing that God is our only source of peace.

It is difficult to keep our eyes on God and our mind steadfastly focused on him. We live in a world with so many distractions—so many problems—that it takes deliberate effort and discipline to train our minds to focus on him rather than on our problems.

How do we learn to focus on God rather than our circumstances? It all comes down to daily reading, knowing, and applying his Word and spending time with him in prayer. I am surer of this than anything else in life.

As long as we live on this earth we will have problems, heartaches, and disappointments. Until we learn that we cannot face those challenges alone in our own power, we are destined to lose our battles and walk in defeat rather than in the victory that is ours in Christ. The Bible tells us that "the LORD longs to be gracious to you; he rises to show you compassion. For the LORD is a God of justice. Blessed are all those who wait for him!" (Isaiah 30:18). The key here is that we must wait for God. We must look for him, and we must wait for him. He alone is able to provide the peace we seek. No man or woman can. No amount of money or achievement can. No amount of human reasoning can. Only God can provide peace in our troubled times.

Our greatest ally in this daily fight to achieve peace and joy is the Word of God. Make this the year that you seek a deeper knowledge and closer walk with God through his Word. I promise you that if you will spend even a few minutes daily laying your needs before him and looking to his Word rather than this world for the answers to your problems, you will encounter God in ways you never dreamed possible.

God loves you and cares deeply about you, enough that he sent his only Son to die on the cross for your sins so that you would have unlimited access to his throne of grace and a relationship with him for all eternity. God is personal, and he promises peace to those who will seek him and put their trust in him.

Does finding God mean your problems will go away? Probably not. But he will walk with you through your valley and comfort you with his presence (Psalm 23:4). His goodness and love will follow you all the days of your life (v. 6).

Rather than focus on your problems, pick up your Bible and begin focusing on God. He is there, his Word is true, his promises are real, and he is faithful to those who choose to believe in him.

WON'T YOU BE MY NEIGHBOR?

Love the Lord your God with all your heart and with all your soul and with all your mind and with all your strength. Love your neighbor as yourself.
Mark 12:30–31

Some of my strangest thoughts come to me at the kitchen sink. As I rinsed the suds down the drain after washing dishes, I thought of Fred Rogers. You know, Mr. Rogers with the great cardigans and the quirky little friends? I miss Mr. Rogers; I learned a lot of important lessons from him. One of the lessons I learned as a little girl, which I find handy even today, is that one can more easily rinse those leftover suds down the drain using cold water rather than hot or warm. I'm sure there is a scientific reason why

Dee Dee Wike

that is so, but that isn't important. Nonetheless, every time I rinse down the suds, I think of wise old Fred.

Mr. Rogers had a way of making us feel good about ourselves, didn't he? Even when others could make us feel lower than a pregnant ant. Don't you love the way he looked into the camera and told you just how special you were? How much you mattered? The truth is, Mr. Rogers was absolutely right. You see, Mr. Rogers could say that because he was a child of God just like we are. He knew the truth about love and acceptance, and he was a master at conveying that to all of us.

Who is your neighbor? Who is that person who needs to know they are loved? As you go about the rest of your week, seek out those persons—perhaps they actually live in your neighborhood—and let them know how special they are to God and to you. If you see a neighbor in need, don't be like the priest and the Levite who walked on the other side of the street. Be a good Samaritan and go out of your way to extend the love of Christ and help your fellow man.

ONE DAY AT A TIME

Therefore do not worry about tomorrow, for tomorrow will worry about itself. Each day has enough trouble of its own.

Matthew 6:34

With all the challenges we face day in and day out, the only way we will survive with our sanity intact is by taking things one day at a time. No matter how much we pray or how hard we try to walk in obedience to God's Word, there will always be a test just around the corner!

When we set our plans for each day, often we do so knowing there will be more on our plates than we can handle. Whether it's working at our jobs, chauffeuring our children to their activities, or taking care of necessary household responsibilities, we will always have more to do than we can comfortably manage in our own strength.

Dee Dee Wike

God is faithful. He knows what we're up against, and he promises to be with us through it all. As we lean on Scripture to carry us through the day, let us find strength in the words of Isaiah 33:6: "He will be the sure foundation for your times, a rich store of salvation and wisdom and knowledge; the fear of the LORD is the key to this treasure." What consolation to know that when the rest of the world seems shaky, God is our sure foundation!

It is not up to us to make sure that all our needs are met and our problems are solved. Rather, it is our privilege and responsibility to seek God first—God and his righteousness—knowing that all the wisdom and provision and grace we need to make it through each day will be given to us as we need it (Matthew 6:33).

By keeping our eyes on God and claiming the promises of his Word to carry us through, we can joyfully face whatever comes our way knowing that he has everything under control.

TONGUE-TIED

> We all stumble in many ways. If anyone is never at
> fault in what he says, he is a perfect man, able to
> keep his whole body in check.
>
> James 3:2

Every now and then, the Lord convicts me about some of
the things I say in jest about my dear husband. Although
my words are not meant to be unkind, they are in truth
hurtful to him, especially when they are said in the presence of our children. What I say as a joke is often received
as disrespect or criticism.

In James 3, we are taught a great deal about the tongue.
James says:

> The tongue is a small part of the body, but it makes
> great boasts. The tongue also is a fire, a world of
> evil among the parts of the body. It corrupts the

whole person, sets the whole course of his life on fire, and is itself set on fire by hell. No man can tame the tongue. It is a restless evil, full of deadly poison. With the tongue we praise our Lord and Father, and with it we curse men, who have been made in God's likeness. Out of the same mouth come praise and cursing.

James 3:5–6; 8–10

As I consider the things that come out of my mouth on a daily basis, I realize that God needs to wash my mouth out with soap, and I need to be a little more tongue-tied. I also know that I need to examine my heart. Based on what I say, it is anything but clean.

Jesus said:

For out of the overflow of the heart the mouth speaks. The good man brings good things out of the good stored up in him, and the evil man brings evil things out of the evil stored up in him. But I tell you that men will have to give account on the day of judgment for every careless word they have spoken. For by your words you will be acquitted, and by your words you will be condemned.

Matthew 12:34–37

As one who cherishes God's Word and realizes the power of the written and spoken word, I know that I need to choose my words a little more carefully if I want to impact others in a positive way. I need to be less critical, especially of my family, and more prone to praise God and others for their positive attributes.

May God make us sensitive to the things that proceed out of our mouths, make us swift to listen and slow to speak. May we choose our words carefully and speak only that which is edifying to God and to others.

CLOSE TO HOME

For I know the plans I have for you, declares the
Lord, plans to prosper you and not harm you,
plans to give you a hope and a future.

Jeremiah 29:11

Several months ago, my brother lost his job in the con-
struction industry because of the economy. He and his
family were no doubt shaken by this change, but they
knew God was unshakable and able to do immeasurably
more than they could ask or imagine (Ephesians 3:20).
They were confident that God would provide for their
needs according to his riches in glory in Christ Jesus
(Philippians 4:19).

We live in world of uncertainty where things often
happen a little "close to home." Our only hope of remaining calm in the midst of all the chaos and of dealing with
the hard blows life deals us is to remember that we are

children of a loving heavenly Father who has engraved us in the palm of his hand (Isaiah 49:16). God is never surprised by the unexpected things that happen to his children. He is sovereign, and he knows everything. God is trustworthy and faithful, owns the cattle on a thousand hills (Psalm 50:10), and is quite capable of providing for his own. In fact, he promises to meet the daily needs of those who will seek him first (Matthew 6:33–34).

If ever there is a time when we need to turn back to God, to fully commit our lives to him, and to trust him for every need of our lives, it is now. We live in a day and age where it is impossible to make it on our own. I don't even want to try because I know how badly I'll mess things up. I fully trust in God's ability to guide, direct, and provide for me and my family.

My prayer for my brother, and for all who might be going through difficult challenges, is that we will allow God to shape us as a result of our difficult circumstances and use us to encourage others in similar situations. God sometimes redirects the course of our lives through changes not of our own making. If we will yield ourselves to his plan, seek his will, and let him be God, then he will work all things together for our good (Romans 8:28).

THE LITTLE THINGS

Do not be like them, for your Father knows what
you need before you ask him.

Matthew 6:8

God often uses the little, and sometimes unusual, things
in life to teach us about his great care and provision for
us. Such was the case for me when I went to buy shower
hooks one day.

While working for the music ministry of my church,
I was charged with the task of ordering curtains from an
out-of-state hospital curtain manufacturer so we could
partition off a section of our women's robe room for costume storage. Finding the curtains was no problem. The
facilities supervisor was even able to use standard metal
pipes to build a frame of heavy-duty rods to hang the
massive curtain panels on once they were ordered. The
challenge for me was simple: find heavy-duty shower

hooks sufficient to bear the weight of the curtains without spending a lot of money in the process.

The curtain panels were large and had many grommets. Because I didn't unpack the curtains and count the number, I had no idea how many hooks I would need. I just knew that they would have to be sturdy. I shopped several places, finally ending up at a Wal-Mart, where I found exactly the kind of hook that would slide easily over the pipes and be sturdy enough to support the weight of the fabric, but I still didn't know how many to buy. Saying a simple prayer for this tiny little detail, I simply bought every package on the rack and headed back to the church to install the curtains. As God would have it, and only he could have known, I had purchased exactly the number of hooks needed to hang the panels. I was absolutely giddy with delight that he had supplied exactly what I needed at the lowest possible price.

Don't be afraid to ask our God for help with the little things in life. He is as concerned with grommets and shower hooks as he is with some of the larger things we face. His love is constant, his provision is sufficient, and his grace is amazing. Ask him for what you need, no matter how insignificant or silly it seems. If it is a big thing to you, then you can know that it matters to him.

STOP, LOOK
AND LISTEN

If you have any encouragement from being united with Christ, if any comfort from his love, if any fellowship with the Spirit, if any tenderness and compassion, then make my joy complete by being like-minded, having the same love, being one in spirit and purpose. Do nothing out of selfish ambition or vain conceit, but in humility consider others better than yourselves.

Philippians 2:1–3

The other day I bumped into a neighbor who was out walking. Although I had chatted briefly with this woman a few times in the past, I decided this time to actually stop what I was doing and make a real effort to learn her name and a little more about her. Knowing what little I already did about her challenges, I thought a little conversation might encourage her. Little did I know that my decision to lay aside my own agenda for a few minutes would turn into an opportunity for ministry and result in my own encouragement.

God often gives us opportunities to encourage and show others his love, but only if we are willing to take the time to stop and listen to those who are hurting or in need. All too often we allow our busyness, insecurities, and self-centeredness to keep us from investing in the lives of others in a meaningful way that could ultimately result in their salvation or healing.

The next time you bump into an individual whose face is familiar, take the encounter to the next level by asking that person his or her name. Make it your mission to get to know that person just a little better with each encounter and ask God to use you as a channel of his love and grace. Whether it is a cashier, bank teller, or the person who sells you donuts on Saturday morning, make it a point to smile and speak a word of encouragement.

God's greatest desire is that others come to a personal, saving knowledge of his Son. He counts on us who already know Jesus to be his instruments of grace and healing to the lost and hurting. Purpose this year to invest a little more of yourself in the lives of others that they may see Christ in you and be drawn into a relationship with him. The dividends you receive will be greater than even you can imagine.

JUST LIKE ME

We have different gifts, according to the grace given us. If a man's gift is prophesying, let him use it in proportion to his faith. If it is serving, let him serve; if it is teaching, let him teach; if it is encouraging, let him encourage; if it is contributing to the needs of others, let him give generously; if it is leadership, let him govern diligently; if it is showing mercy, let him do it cheerfully.

Romans 12:6–8

After an especially stressful week with family and school obligations, I attended a Sunday school ladies' fellowship at the home of one of our members. Our pastor's wife was the guest speaker. After she spoke on the fruit of the Spirit, she gave us each a bracelet with one bead and asked what one thing—fruit, spiritual gift, etc.—it was that we needed to put on and claim as our own. After praying with a partner, we each shared with the group the one thing we needed.

For me, it was patience—not only with others, but also with myself. For others, it was things such as love, peace, perseverance, and so on. As I listened to these ladies share their needs, I realized that I was not alone. The other ladies were pretty much like me, each struggling with her own issues. We were able to encourage one another simply by listening, sharing, and praying together.

God knows that the challenges we face are sometimes overwhelming. He does not intend for us to face them alone. We are called to carry each other's burdens and thus fulfill the law of Christ (Galatians 6:2). Not only are we to carry each other's burdens, sometimes we also need to share our own challenges. Scripture tells us that God comforts us in our troubles so that we can comfort others going through similar challenges (2 Corinthians 1:4). Sometimes we simply need to know that there are others just like us.

Whatever your challenges are today, know that there are others around you going through challenges of their own and needing encouragement just as you do. Rather than focus on and be discouraged by your own struggles, offer a word of encouragement to someone who needs a gentle reminder that they're not alone and that others really do care about and understand the challenges they face. As you encourage someone else, you will lighten his burden and find yours not quite so heavy to bear.

LEAVING THE PAST BEHIND

But one thing I do: Forgetting what is behind and straining toward what is ahead, I press on toward the goal to win the prize for which God has called me heavenward in Christ Jesus.

Philippians 3:13–14

As each year draws to a close, we look back on all that happened during the current year and make goals and resolutions for the year ahead. We long to leave behind the pain of yesterday and embrace a happier tomorrow. We hope that the year ahead will be one of better health, greater prosperity, and more joy. Eager to lay aside the heartaches, relationship challenges, and financial hardship that have characterized many of our lives this past year, we resolve to press on to new beginnings and successful ventures, pouring our resources and energy into achieving our personal goals, meeting new friends, and experiencing new adventures.

Sadly, we attempt to do many of these things in our own power without inviting God to be an active participant in our daily lives. Perhaps that is why we fail to break free from the past and move on to the gloriously abundant life that awaits those who follow Christ.

If we closely examine our lives, we will see behavioral patterns that lead to the misery that seems to perpetuate itself. For those of us who call ourselves Christians, the real danger lies in living life on our own terms rather than in obedience to God's Word. When we dabble in sin, as innocent as some sins may appear, we unwittingly fetter ourselves to the very strongholds we are trying to break. By neglecting the spiritual disciplines of studying God's Word, communicating with him in prayer, and serving others, we run the risk of becoming self-absorbed and missing out on the true joy of being God's children.

Many years ago, I decided to trade in the mediocrity of my self-centered existence for the great adventure of a Christ-centered life. It is a decision I have never regretted. Sure, there have been times when I have sinned by succumbing to temptation or giving God less than my best. But he has been quick to convict me of my sins, even quicker to forgive me, and willing to pick me up, brush me off, and point me in the right direction. I have learned to trust him through the most difficult challenges, to love him more deeply in the lonely times, and to lean on his grace and strength each and every day. My life is

Dee Dee Wike

not any easier than when I walked apart from him, but the sweetness of his presence has brought a joy to my life that no person, achievement, or possession ever has.

God has a great plan for your life. He wants you to leave your painful past behind and venture into a joyful and fulfilling future with him. Begin today by recommitting your life to his perfect will for you, spending time daily in his Word, talking with him often, and serving others rather than yourself. If you will purpose to walk in obedience and do all things for his glory alone, you will find yourself living a life with no regrets.

DOGS EATING FIGS

A cheerful heart is good medicine, but a crushed spirit dries up the bones.

Proverbs 17:22

While on Facebook one day, I noticed that a friend of mine had taken one of the many quizzes on the site, which posted the following cause of death: "Died of laughter after watching your drunk dog eat figs." (This is precisely why I don't do Facebook quizzes. I'm absolutely terrified of what any computer might say about me.) That quirky status elicited a chuckle or two and an off-the-wall comment from me, which resulted in a challenge from her to write a blog about dogs eating figs. I don't know that I will ever see dogs eating figs, but the image it conjures up in my mind is quite hilarious, and these days I can use a good laugh.

Dee Dee Wike

My family and I sat down recently and watched an absolutely idiotic movie (so idiotic that I refuse to say what it was). I don't know when I have laughed so hard. Just hearing my husband and daughter hee-haw uncontrollably made me laugh even harder. By the time the movie ended, we were nearly wheezing from having laughed so much. I don't know which was more pathetic: all our silliness or the movie itself.

Life becomes so stressful at times that we simply forget to laugh. I know an awful lot of long-faced Christians who look like poster children for unhappiness. The Bible tells us that a cheerful heart is good medicine. The next time you feel the need for a pill or a drink to cheer you up, try a little laughter instead. It's cheap, it's effective, and it's non-toxic. Even better, share your laughter with someone else. Laughter can be highly contagious. God knows the world could use an epidemic of joy.

BE IT UNTO ME

Let it be done for you according to your faith!

Matthew 9:29, HCSB

God must have a pretty full plate these days listening to and handling all the prayer requests that come his way. I know I send him enough to keep him busy. Although prayer is not just about making our requests known to God, it is good to know that he hears our prayers and answers them when we pray according to his will and believe that he is able to do what we have asked of him.

In the ninth chapter of Matthew, we find the story of Jesus healing two blind men who had been following him.

> When he had gone indoors, the blind men came to him, and he asked them, "Do you believe that I am able to do this?" "Yes, Lord," they replied. Then he touched their eyes and said, "According

Dee Dee Wike

to your faith it will be done to you"; and their sight was restored.

Matthew 9:28–30

When you pray, do you honestly believe God is able to do those things you ask of him, such as provide for your daily needs, heal your diseases, and restore your broken relationships? Do you acknowledge that you are unable to do these things for yourself and place your hope in his ability to answer your prayers? When you pray, are you praying for things that are consistent with God's will?

In Matthew 6:9–13, Jesus teaches us how to pray by giving us an example commonly referred to as the Lord's Prayer. Most of us are familiar with that prayer, but how many of us pray according to Christ's example? Rather than begin my prayer time acknowledging God's holiness, praising him for his attributes, confessing my sins, and thanking him for his goodness, I tend to just jump right in with a laundry list of prayer requests. I'll bet you do too. I don't think any of us can improve on Christ's example, so why don't we pray like him more often?

After the angel visited Mary to tell her that she would be the mother of our Lord, her response was, "Be it unto me according to thy word" (Luke 1:38, KJV). That is how we all must pray—from a position of submission to God's will and with confidence in the power of his Word to accomplish his purpose in our lives.

FINDING JOY AND PEACE IN THE BITTER BATTLE

Get rid of all bitterness, rage and anger, brawling
and slander, along with every form of malice. Be
kind and compassionate to one another, forgiving
each other, just as in Christ God forgave you.

Ephesians 4:31–32

Heart disease is not just a physical problem. In many
senses, it is a spiritual and emotional problem as well.
Many of us walk around with physical hearts that are just
fine, but we are brokenhearted on the inside—brokenhearted and bitter.

Life is brutal. Because of financial worries compounded by a deteriorating economy, the deaths of those close to us, devastating illness, and the dysfunction of our relationships with family and friends, it seems we are destined to a life of bitterness and sorrow. You could say that each of us has a darn good reason to be angry with others, with ourselves, and with God.

God didn't promise any of us that life would be easy or free of heartbreak. On the contrary, Jesus himself said, "I have told you these things, so that in me you may have peace. In this world you will have trouble. But take heart! I have overcome the world" (John 16:33). If God told us there would be trouble, then why should any of us be surprised by the problems we face day in and day out?

You don't have to look far to see the walking wounded around you. All of us have problems that at times seem insurmountable. We are weary and battle scarred. But then, we live in a battle zone. Those of us who are Christians are engaged in spiritual warfare, and Satan is relentless in his attacks and efforts to defeat us in our walk with Christ. His primary weapon against us, I'm convinced, is our own family. If there is anything that can harden our hearts and keep us from experiencing the true joy and peace of our relationship with God, it's the constant wounding of our hearts by our families and those closest to us.

How do we fight and win a battle that seems so hopeless? And what exactly is the prize we are fighting so hard to win? Clearly, the prize is peace—peace in our troubled relationships and peace with ourselves. How do we move beyond the bitterness and despair and find that peace?

Ultimately, we find our peace by knowing and trusting the one who *is* our peace. Isaiah 26:3–4 assures us, "You will keep in perfect peace him whose mind is steadfast, because he trusts in you. Trust in the LORD forever, for the LORD, the LORD, is the Rock eternal."

Jesus, though fully God, was also fully man; therefore, he suffered many of the same things we do. It is written,

> For we do not have a high priest who is unable to sympathize with our weaknesses, but we have one who has been tempted in every way, just as we are—yet was without sin. Let us then approach the throne of grace with confidence, so that we may receive mercy and find grace to help us in our time of need.
>
> Hebrews 4:15–16

Jesus understands the sting of rejection, for he was rejected. He understands temptation and anger and hurt, for he experienced all of them. Yet he never lost sight of his relationship with the Father, the true anchor for his soul. Neither must we lose sight.

Jesus forgave our sins for all eternity when he died on the cross for our salvation. He expects us to also forgive those who have sinned against us. In fact, Jesus tells us that if we don't forgive others, God will not forgive us (Matthew 6:14–15). It is not enough to say that we have forgiven someone else; we must mean it. In forgiving them, we must let go of the hurt, or we will never be released from our bitterness.

Who is it that you need to forgive today? A spouse, a child, yourself? The only way you can find your way back to the peace and joy that God promises you is by forgiving those who have offended you and allowing God to heal and soften your heart toward others. If we look to others to supply our joy and peace, we will come up disappointed. No human being can supply the joy that Christ can. But our bitterness toward others can steal our joy and rob us of the peace that Christ has promised us.

Satan wants to keep you in bondage. He will never stop sending irritating people, distractions, and discouragement your way. He doesn't fight fair. You, however, have weapons at your disposal far greater than anything he wields, and you have Almighty God on your side (Romans 8:31). "For though we live in the world, we do not wage war as the world does. The weapons we fight with are not the weapons of the world. On the contrary, they have divine power to demolish strongholds" (2 Corinthians 10:3–4).

Your most effective weapons to fight and prevent spiritual heart disease are the Word of God and prayer. The ultimate cure, though, is a relationship with Jesus. He is not just a historical figure. He is Almighty God, and he is ready to fight for you. Do you know him? Have you made him your Savior? If not, trust him today, ask him into your heart, read and study his Word, and know that all you need—every solution, every provision, all wisdom and grace—can be found in him.

LOVING THAT NEW CAR SMELL

For we are to God the aroma of Christ among those who are being saved and those who are perishing. To the one we are the smell of death; to the other, the fragrance of life. And who is equal to such a task? Unlike so many, we do not peddle the Word of God for profit. On the contrary, in Christ we speak before God with sincerity, like men sent from God.

2 Corinthians 2:15–17

It has been years since I have owned a new car, and I find myself a bit envious of those sporting a shiny new ride. There is nothing quite like that new car smell. Come to think of it, there are many aromas that tickle my nose in a most pleasant way: the smell of fresh-brewed coffee, the

Dee Dee Wike

fragrance of a spring rain, and an infant that has just been bathed and lathered with baby lotion. Those of us who are cooped up in offices or factories all day relish that first breath of fresh air as we step outside and make our way home in the evening.

We live in a world that is polluted not only with vehicle emissions and factory wastes but also the effects of sin. Even the people around us can make us feel dirty by their words and actions. Many Christians are so busy conforming to this world that they are no longer the breath of fresh air that our world so desperately needs. Instead, we often reek of sin because we continue to wallow in the same bad choices and behaviors that everyone else is making these days.

The Bible tells us that we are to be the aroma of Christ among those with whom we live, work, and play. The only way to achieve that is to live out authentic Christianity by walking in obedience to the Word of God. It is impossible to be a breath of fresh air to those around us if we are no different than they are. The only thing that can set us apart is the love of Christ manifested in us and our commitment to follow him in complete surrender.

When you walk into a room or engage in conversation with someone else today, will you be the same old stale person or a breath of fresh air to them? Before you leave home, don't just take a good look at yourself in the mirror; take a good whiff as well. If you smell the stench of your own sin, confess it to Jesus and ask him to wash you clean. Only then can you be the aroma of Christ among those who are perishing.

GETTING THE HELP WE NEED

Dear friend, I pray that you may enjoy good health
and that all may go well with you, even as your
soul is getting along well.

3 John 2

There has long been a stigma attached to depression and
treatment of the condition, especially in Christian circles.
A couple of years ago, what had once been mild, short-
lived depression became a problem I couldn't seem to
resolve on my own or through prayer, so I decided to do
something about it. My symptoms—sleeplessness, occasional anxiety, and a real sense of sadness over a personal
loss—surfaced, I believe, because of hormonal changes
common to women my age. A physical exam and a couple of counseling sessions with a Christian psychologist

helped me to better understand what was going on in my body and with my emotions and started me on the path to healing. Although my depression did not warrant drug therapy, I did take prescribed sleep medication for a period of time. I am now sleeping peacefully again and taking proactive steps to help myself during those times when I feel out of balance physically and emotionally.

Depression has long been viewed as a weakness in Christians. In reality, many of the characters we read of in the Bible suffered from depression and dysfunction. King David comes to mind as one who was at times plagued by sadness and anxiety. The Psalms are full of passages where David pours out his heart to God in sorrow and anger, and others where he praises God for all his goodness. I think we need to understand that depression is a very real condition, that it is not uncommon, and that seeking treatment is nothing to be ashamed of.

If you or someone you know suffers from depression, pray for them. Encourage them in the Lord and with Scripture. But most of all, help them learn about depression and encourage them to seek medical help if needed. God wants his children to be healthy, physically and emotionally, and to enjoy the life of abundance that is ours in Christ.

A DOLLAR SAVED IS
A LESSON LEARNED

She is like the merchant ships, bringing her food
from afar.

Proverbs 31:14

One afternoon, I went grocery shopping for the first time
in weeks. Money had been tight for months so I had been
spending only what was absolutely necessary to feed my
family one day at a time. We were out of nearly everything, so I went shopping with the goal of stocking up
on essentials to get us through the next couple of weeks.
Because I was determined to spend only the cash I had on
hand, I had to shop very carefully and go where the bar-
gains were, which meant that I had to drive into town and
shop at five different stores. By the grace of God, I had

just enough cash to pay for everything (a *huge* victory for someone trying not to use credit cards) and enough time to complete my errands before picking up my daughter from her friend's house.

Isn't it funny how being short on cash makes one a little more careful when shopping? I have found that because I have less to spend when I do go out shopping, we eat a little less and are more conscious of the nutritional value of the food we buy. I am learning that there are healthy alternatives to pizza and hamburgers from fast-food restaurants. Granted, I have to spend a little more time shopping because I can't simply run in and out of Wal-Mart to get everything on my list, but the extra effort to save here and there pays off.

If we ever truly realize that everything we have comes from God's hands, then perhaps we will become better and more creative stewards of his provision and give generously to those with needs greater than our own. Just like managing money requires effort and discipline, giving to those in need costs us time and money. But the dividends we will receive in return for giving will far outweigh the cost!

UNKNOWN

O LORD, you have searched me and you know
me. You know when I sit and when I rise; you
perceive my thoughts from afar. You discern my
going out and my lying down; you are familiar
with all my ways.

Psalm 139:1–3

One Sunday, our pastor preached on relationships, specifically our relationships with one another in the body of
Christ. It was a powerful message brought to life in an especially meaningful way by the testimony of a young woman
in our church. As she shared the heart-wrenching experiences she suffered prior to finding and accepting Jesus as
her Savior, I thought back over my own life and the many
things I have been hesitant to share about my own journey.

We all have experiences—skeletons in our closet—that
we are hesitant to share with others for fear of offending

or being rejected by the people we know. Certainly that is true in my life. But nothing is hidden from God. He knew us before we were conceived, and all the days ordained for us were written before one of them came to be (Psalm 139:15–16).

I have done some shameful things in my life and have experienced a great deal of pain and sorrow. Although I don't routinely share the painful secrets of my past, there are times when God leads me to open up to others. When that happens, I never cease to be amazed at how God uses the pain of my past to minister to someone else. Even my worst mistakes can be a blessing if I allow God to take and use them for his glory.

Although I might offend some, nothing in my past can overshadow the unconditional love that God has for me. In Romans 8:1, the Apostle Paul writes, "Therefore, there is now no condemnation for those who are in Christ Jesus, because through Christ Jesus the law of the Spirit of life set me free from the law of sin and death." Praise you, Jesus!

What is the secret that you are keeping buried deep inside? Don't let fear keep you from sharing the one thing that might reach another lost or needy soul! There are people in your circle of influence who need to know that the loving God who healed you from your shameful past can heal them from theirs.

EMBRACING CHANGE

Jesus Christ is the same yesterday and today and forever.

Hebrews 13:8

On the day we inaugurated our nation's forty-fourth president, most of us were filled with anticipation and some of us with anxiety over the changes that were promised during his campaign. Not only was history made as we elected our first African-American president, but we faced an uncertain political and economic climate, holding on to every hope that the changes to come would be positive ones.

As Christians, we should be filled with anticipation and hope each and every day of our lives. We should eagerly expect the return of our King, the one who sits on the throne. We should live our lives with certainty that he is in control of our destiny and that our future is secure because God reigns.

It is our duty as God's soldiers in the fierce spiritual battle that rages daily to stand on the front line of this war and fight for the values that he established in his Word. We are to know his Word and be clad with the spiritual armor of God (Ephesians 6:13–18).

It is our duty to pray for and support our new president, whether or not we elected him (Romans 13:1). Like any person, President Obama is a man with a heart and soul, and he will need the same divine guidance that each of us seek as we wage war against our true enemy.

As we embrace new leadership, we must be careful not to embrace any change that is inconsistent with God's holy standards for his people. We must continue to fight for what is right and stand against those things that are wrong in the sight of our Lord.

BEAUTIFUL FEET

How beautiful are the feet of those who bring good news!

Romans 10:15

Like so many other Americans, I spent much of Inauguration Day watching news coverage of the festivities in Washington. One thing that impressed me was how much activity was crammed into that historic day. Just seeing First Lady Michelle Obama on her feet so much made me thankful that I am not in her shoes, literally! Can you even imagine how tired her feet must have been by the time she made it to the Inaugural Ball? I live in tennis shoes, so most days my feet don't get tired. But on those days when they do, I wish I could simply remove my feet.

The Bible talks about feet and shoes (sandals). We are told in Romans 10 that those who bring the good news of the gospel have beautiful feet (v. 15). In God's

Dee Dee Wike

eyes, those who know, love, and serve him are beautiful from head to toe.

When Moses encountered God at the burning bush, the Lord said, "Do not come any closer. Take off your sandals, for the place where you are standing is holy ground" (Exodus 3:5). There have been times when I have walked away from a situation, such as an opportunity to minister to someone else, that I have literally felt as if I had been standing on holy ground. God will use us if we make ourselves available to him and allow him to accomplish his purposes in and through us. There is no greater feeling than to know that God has used you to touch the heart of another.

In Matthew 3, John the Baptist declared, "I baptize you with water for repentance. But after me will come one who is more powerful than I, whose sandals I am not fit to carry. He will baptize you with the Holy Spirit and with fire" (v. 11). Who of us is fit to serve our great God? None of us is worthy except by his amazing grace. We certainly cannot fill the shoes of Christ, who humbled himself and became a servant of mankind, but we can serve as his feet by proclaiming the good news of his salvation in our circles of influence.

What is the condition of your feet? Are they bare because you have been in the presence of the Lord and beautiful because you are busily proclaiming his truth and salvation to others? Are you eager to put on your running shoes and run the race so as to win the prize (1 Corinthians 9:24)? Or are they weary from walking beneath a load of care? As you allow Jesus to come alongside you and carry your burden, he will give you strength to keep putting one foot in front of the other as you serve others for his glory. Oh, what a wonderful God we serve. May our feet be beautiful and our faces reflect his glory as we step out and serve those who walk beside us each day.

SEPARATION ANXIETY

For I am convinced that neither death nor life, neither angels nor demons, neither the present nor the future, nor any powers, neither height nor depth, nor anything else in all creation, will be able to separate us from the love of God that is in Christ Jesus our Lord.

Romans 8:38

Since the beginning of time, God has separated things. On day one of creation, he separated light from darkness. On day two, he created a space (the sky) to separate the waters above the earth from the waters under the earth. Both times, the separations were for a particular reason, resulting in the distinction between night and day and the formation of ground so he could supply food for us

(Genesis 1:11-12). In both cases, the Bible tells us, "God saw that it was good." Why is it, then, that we become anxious when separation makes its way into our lives?

The past couple of years have been ones of absolute joy and adventure for me, despite the challenges I faced as a homeschool mom. During the time we had together as homeschoolers, my son and I grew closer and developed a bond that has helped us weather the stormy sea of adolescence. He reentered the school system at the beginning of the 2009–2010 school year and has done well despite all the challenges of being a modern-day teen. God allowed me a few extra months with my daughter to strengthen our bond and prepare us both for the journey ahead of us. Knowing that God is in control and has great things in store for both of us helped minimize any separation anxiety we felt as I re-enrolled her in school after Christmas.

Separation is seldom easy. When we are separated from the people and activities we love so much, we grieve our loss, sometimes without even realizing it. We spend so much time and effort worrying about what will come as a result of the separation that we often don't see the benefit of it. But there can be great blessing in separation if we allow God to draw us to him and have his way in us.

If you are facing separation of any kind, ask God to show you what is on the other side and to give you the courage to walk through your challenge, hand in hand with him. He will not leave you. Nothing that comes into your life can separate you from his love. If you are facing the loss of a job, he will provide for your daily needs (Philippians 4:19). Trust him. If you find yourself suddenly

Dee Dee Wike

alone, he will be with you to comfort and keep you. Know that in all things God is working things together for your good (Romans 8:28).

AN EVER-PRESENT HELP

God is our refuge and strength, an ever-present help in trouble. Therefore we will not fear, though the earth give way and the mountains fall into the heart of the sea, though its waters roar and foam and the mountains quake with their surging.

Psalm 46:1–3

As I began my prayer time, my journal entry went something like this:

My mind is thinking about a dozen things right now—the blog I want to write, the book I want to see published, the book I am writing now, my decision to leave one ministry in order to participate in another, the announcement by my husband's employer that it posted a $6.24 billion loss in the fourth quarter, and how that might affect his job and our finances. Lord, I'm so glad I'm not on this journey alone. You are with me, an ever-present help in times of trouble.

As I thought about all these things, the one thing I kept coming back to was the assurance that God was in control of every aspect of my life and that I had no reason to fear.

I know that with each challenge God allows to flow into my life, even greater will be the grace, wisdom, and provision he will supply to face those challenges. His Word promises me everything I need to live confidently, expectantly, and victoriously.

I know that my husband could be handed a pink slip this very day or that some other devastating event could take place, but I do not fear what the future holds because I know the God who holds my future. He knows the plans that he has for me (Jeremiah 29:11), and he knows the way that I take (Job 23:10). "And we know that in all things God works for the good of those who love him, who have been called according to his purpose" (Romans 8:28).

We live in a world that is anything but peaceful. With the economy in its present decline, the health issues many of us face, and the pervasive uncertainty that is simply part of living in our culture at this time in history, we need the refuge and strength only God can provide through a relationship with his Son, Jesus.

FEEDING THE DOG WITHIN

But just as he who called you is holy, so be holy
in all you do; for it is written: "Be holy, because I
am holy."

1 Peter 1:15–16

As a teenage new believer many years ago, I heard a
story, which has greatly impacted my walk with the Lord
through the years. Although I can't remember the source,
the truth was and is still profound, at least to me.

The story was told of a man who had two dogs, a good
dog and a bad dog. When asked the question, "In a fight,
which dog will win?" the man replied, "Whichever dog I
feed." How much better can a story illustrate the struggle
between good and evil, or said another way, the Spirit-
filled life versus a sinful life lived in the flesh?

In our society, we don't have to look far to find influences that would corrupt our thinking, compromise our values, or cause us to walk in a manner unbefitting a child of God. Present-day media inundates us with visual images, words, and ideas that are contrary to God's Word and his holy standard for us.

The mind is a battlefield, and what we place in our minds quite often determines what our actions will be. For instance, there are certain recording artists I no longer listen to because their songs conjure up memories of my college years when I was out of fellowship with the Lord and engaged in habitual sin. Those old behaviors lie just beneath the surface now, and I know that at any time I could fall if I don't consciously guard against the tendency to entertain thoughts that could lead to sinful behavior.

The Bible says:

> Finally, brothers, whatever is true, whatever is noble, whatever is right, whatever is pure, whatever is lovely, whatever is admirable—if anything is excellent or praiseworthy—think about these things.
>
> Philippians 4:8

If we are to think about "these things," we must know what they are. We must read and meditate on the Scriptures, learn God's truths about sinful and righteous living, and act on those truths rather than live according to the world's value system.

You have a choice to make. Which dog are you going to feed?

THIS LIFE IS NOT ALL THERE IS

I consider that our present sufferings are not worth
comparing with the glory that will be revealed in us.
Romans 8:18

The year may be young and full of promise for many of
us, but for some it has dawned with burdens too heavy to
bear. Several of my closest friends are dealing with heart-
wrenching circumstances over which they have little, if
any, control. Just in the past few weeks, a handful of them
have learned that their cancer has returned. Others are
dealing with family situations involving prodigal children,
drug addiction, or the loss of a spouse. Many are reeling
from financial problems as a result of job loss, the down-
turn in our economy, or catastrophic illness.

Although I know that God is in control of everything that affects our lives, lately I have seen the suffer-

ing of many escalate and wondered, "Lord, what is going on? Why is everything suddenly falling apart for those I love?" The answer is simple, really. We live in a fallen world where men are corrupt, people die, and Satan does everything in his power to turn us away from the loving God who is himself our peace (Ephesians 2:14). All the while we eagerly look forward to the return of our Savior, knowing well that we are living in the last days and none of these adversities should take us by surprise.

> But mark this: There will be terrible times in the last days. People will be lovers of themselves, lovers of money, boastful, proud, abusive, disobedient to their parents, ungrateful, unholy, without love, unforgiving, slanderous, without self-control, brutal, not lovers of the good.
>
> 2 Timothy 3:1–3

Jesus himself said that we would have trouble in this world (John 16:33), but he also promised that he is preparing a place for us in heaven and will come to take us there (John 14:2–3). This world is not all there is.

No matter how difficult your problems may be, if you have a personal relationship with Jesus, you have the hope of a better tomorrow and the assurance that he will be present with you today. You can take joy in knowing that for your loved ones who are nearing the end of their earthly lives to be absent from the body is to be present with the Lord (2 Corinthians 5:8). Does that mean you shouldn't mourn their death or grieve your loss? Certainly you should, but you need not grieve like the rest of men who have no hope.

As Christians, "we believe that Jesus died and rose again and so we believe that God will bring with Jesus those who have fallen asleep in him" (1 Thessalonians 4:13–14). We have the assurance of being reunited with our loved ones who have received Christ as their Savior and the joy of knowing that they are going to heaven, where "there will be no more death or mourning or crying or pain" (Revelation 21:4).

If you hold tightly to these promises from God's Word, there is no challenge you can't face or sorrow you cannot bear. Jesus *is* coming, and when he does, what a day of rejoicing that will be!

I CAN'T FIX THIS!

.

If anyone acknowledges that Jesus is the Son of God, God lives in him and he in God. And so we know and rely on the love God has for us.

1 John 4:15–16

Many of us are fixers. We go about our lives fixing broken this and broken that. Our attempts to repair things like leaky faucets, broken windows, and other items around the house are quite often successful. But how do we repair the broken hearts and shattered lives of the people we live among every day? The truth is, we can't.

I have spent a lifetime, it seems, trying to fix what's wrong with others. Lord knows I haven't exactly been successful fixing what's wrong with *me*, let alone anybody else. Yet that hasn't kept me from trying—time and time again—to get right in there and fix what only God can. All these efforts have led to a lot of codependency issues in my relationships with others.

According to the Merriam-Webster dictionary[1], codependency is defined as "a psychological condition or a relationship in which a person is controlled or manipulated by another who is affected with a pathological condition (as an addiction to alcohol or heroin); broadly: dependence on the needs of or control by another." Many of us can point to codependent relationships we have had with others, often to our detriment emotionally, physically, and spiritually.

If you think about it, much of our codependency is driven by a need for approval and acceptance by people other than God. As we allow God's unconditional love to flow into our lives and we in turn surrender our lives to him, we will become less consumed by the need for continual affirmation by people who have a place of significance in our lives, whether they are family, friends, or coworkers.

Being codependent is miserable. Learning to love ourselves and others because God first loved us (1 John 4:10) is the only way to find healing and wholeness from codependency.

There is only one person I know who can fix what's truly wrong with any of us, and his name is Jesus. His grace is sufficient, his love is unconditional, and his peace and power are available for all who have faith enough to believe in him. He does not mean for any of us to live in emotional poverty or bondage to others; rather, he desires for us to find in him our sufficiency, peace, and delight.

God calls his children to love and serve one another (1 John 3:16–18), but it is not our job to *fix* anybody. That alone is God's job. Ours is to care deeply enough to pray for them and do all in our power to bring them to the Savior (Mark 2:3–5), who alone can forgive our sins and heal our diseases.

Dee Dee Wike

STUMBLING BLOCK OR STEPPING STONE?

You are a stumbling block to me; you do not have
in mind the things of God, but the things of men.
Matthew 16:23

For over thirty years, I have journeyed through this life as
a child of God. I have been through seasons of intimate
fellowship with him as well as seasons of spiritual drought
and sinful living. I have been both deeply moved by things
of the Spirit and negatively influenced by the ungodliness
of our society. The constant struggle to strive for holiness
in a depraved generation has left me weary and battle-
scarred. Like many, I have been a stumbling block rather

than a stepping-stone to those in the church who walk with Christ and those outside of it who are seeking him.

I am convinced that we, as Christians, are not embracing God's call to holiness and living the way he intended. We are living in spiritual poverty rather than the abundant life Christ came to bring us (John 10:10) because we continue to buy into a secular rather than a Christian worldview in so many areas of our lives. In Romans 12, Paul urges the church:

> In view of God's mercy, to offer your bodies as living sacrifices, holy and pleasing to God—this is your spiritual act of worship. Do not conform any longer to the pattern of this world, but be transformed by the renewing of your mind. Then you will be able to test and approve what God's will is—his good, pleasing and perfect will.
>
> Romans 12:1–2

How can we pray for and know God's will and purpose for our lives if we are feeding our minds earthly table scraps rather than feasting on the rich fare of God's Word?

Until we embrace holiness and strive to live our lives according to God's Word, we will never be a stepping-stone to Christ and his salvation for those who are lost and hurting. Our lives *must* be a true reflection of his glory and his character if we are to draw others to Christ and effect positive change in our world.

> Therefore, as God's chosen people, holy and dearly loved, clothe yourselves with compassion,

kindness, humility, gentleness and patience. Bear with each other and forgive whatever grievances you may have against one another. Forgive as the Lord forgave you. And over all these virtues put on love, which binds them all together in perfect unity. Let the word of Christ dwell in you richly... and whatever you do, whether in word or deed, do it all in the name of the Lord Jesus, giving thanks to God the Father through him.

Colossians 3:12–14; 16–17

TO TELL THE TRUTH

Then we will no longer be infants, tossed back and forth by the waves, and blown here and there by every wind of teaching and by the cunning and craftiness of men in their deceitful scheming. Instead, speaking the truth in love, we will in all things grow up into him who is the Head, that is, Christ.

Ephesians 4:14–15

When my nine-year-old lost a tooth, the tooth fairy left her not one, but two golden dollars and an expertly crafted note in an effort to keep his identity a secret. My daughter, however, figured out the truth. She came to me and said, "Mom, I want to ask you something, and I really want to know the truth. Are *you* the tooth fairy?" Her eyes were so entreating, and her desire to know the truth was so sincere that I was compelled to tell her the truth. Next came the *really* big question, "Is Santa Claus real?"

I hedged a little bit. I wasn't sure that I was prepared to tell the truth and risk taking away even a smidgen of her childhood innocence.

We are all aware that sometimes the truth hurts. Yet God calls us to speak the truth in love to those who need to hear it and to live above reproach in every aspect of our lives. God is not the author of lies; in fact, he calls Satan the "father of lies." Deception is not God's character; it is a hallmark of the enemy.

It is easier to tell someone else the truth about their shortcomings than to admit our own faults. Often we are more prone to live a lie than to judge ourselves and walk in the truth. Many of us live with secret sin, areas of our life that we know don't please God. Satan whispers, "It's really not that bad, is it?"

Yet the Spirit within us pleads for us to be truthful about our sin, to confess it, and to repent of it. Only in doing so can we find true freedom and victory. "This then is how we know that we belong to the truth, and how we set our hearts at rest in his presence whenever our hearts condemn us. For God is greater than our hearts, and he knows everything" (1 John 3:19–20). If God already knows everything, then why do we go to such great lengths to hide the truth from him?

Did I tell my daughter the truth about Santa Claus? Yes, I did, despite the fear that by doing so I would hurt her feelings or disillusion her somehow. It was important for her to know, and it was even more important to me and to God that I be truthful with her.

RENEWED

He will not grow tired or weary, and his understanding no one can fathom.

Isaiah 40:28

As I put the wraps on another busy day, I found myself wishing I could say that I don't grow tired or weary. The problem is, most days I am so tired when I fall into bed that I toss and turn in fitful slumber. I'm sure you know exactly what I mean. My friend, Sylvia, tells me my mind never rests, and she is absolutely right about that. Even in my sleep my mind is busy generating all kinds of dreams. Thankfully, they are seldom nightmares. Still, just once I would like to fall asleep and wake up feeling refreshed.

When I awake groggy from a restless night's sleep, I lean heavily on the following verses to strengthen me for the day ahead:

Dee Dee Wike

He gives strength to the weary and increases the power of the weak. Even youths grow tired and weary, and young men stumble and fall; but those who hope in the LORD will renew their strength. They will soar on wings like eagles; they will run and not grow weary, they will walk and not faint.

Isaiah 40:29–31

God's Word absolutely energizes me. Knowing that he understands all there is to know about me—things even I don't understand or want to admit to myself—is something I simply cannot fathom.

How great is our God that he would reveal himself through the pages of his Word, show us everything we need to live a life of purpose, and give us the hope and encouragement to keep putting one foot in front of the other.

"He will keep you strong to the end, so that you will be blameless on the day of our Lord Jesus Christ. God, who has called you into fellowship with his Son Jesus Christ our Lord, is faithful" (1 Corinthians 1:8–9).

RESTORED

Though you have made me see troubles, many and bitter, you will restore my life again; from the depths of the earth you will again bring me up. You will increase my honor and comfort me once again.

Psalm 71:20–21

Next to my relationship with Jesus, my greatest treasure in life is my Bible. God's Word gives me the strength and courage to live in a world where hope has become greatly diminished and godliness is a thing of the past. One of my favorite books of the Bible is Psalms. No other writer in Scripture has a better handle on the complexity of our emotions than King David. I can relate to him on so many levels and find his words to be revealing and relevant, even today.

So many of us walk around dazed and wounded by the affairs of life—our struggle with sin and debilitating sickness, our brokenness over the hurts inflicted on us by others, and our fear of what is to come. The intensity of our present pain obscures any hope we may have of a positive outcome, and we become hopeless and despairing. Yet the Bible is full of hope and assurance that God is aware of our struggles and present with us in them. He knows all that we have been through and everything that we struggle with, and he cares.

When I look back over my life and consider the struggles I have faced along the way, I can't help but rejoice at the way God has used each one to draw me just a little closer to him. He has taken every hurt I have suffered and every mistake I have made and used them to transform my life, and in some cases, minister to others.

I don't think we realize, in the heat of the battle, that God is at work in our lives and that he is refining us through the trials we face. Rather than rely on his Word and draw strength and wisdom from his Holy Spirit, we try to navigate our challenges in our own strength, and as a result, we often stumble and fall. If we will look up, see his face, and take his outstretched hand, he will pull us up, steady our stance, and enable us to continue walking one step at a time.

No matter what struggles you are facing today, God's Word offers you this hope: "And the God of all grace, who called you to his eternal glory in Christ, after you have suffered a little while, will himself restore you and make you strong, firm and steadfast" (1 Peter 5:10).

NO LIMIT

Now all glory to God, who is able, through his mighty power at work within us, to accomplish infinitely more than we might ask or think.

Ephesians 3:20 (NLT)

We all face an uncertain future, but we can face it knowing that our faithful God is in control. No matter what limitations we may see with our earthly eyes, we can know for certain that God is able to do immeasurably more than we can ask or imagine. He is able to tear down the strongholds in our lives, help us change our bad habits, and redeem our mistakes. He is able to provide; in fact, he promises to provide everything we need one day at a time (Philippians 4:19). His ability to provide is not set by a predetermined credit limit; after all, he owns the cattle on a thousand hills (Psalm 50:10). There is no limit to what God can do.

Dee Dee Wike

It is a customary practice to reflect on our dreams and expectations of life as we move through its various seasons, whether as the result of a new job, a major life change, or a simple reallocation of our time and talents. As hard as we try to set our goals and make our plans with God's will in mind, often our vision is hazy, but God's never is. Neither is he constrained by our limitations. He is able to work in and through us by the power of his Holy Spirit, equipping us to do his will and to fulfill his purpose for us.

What is the dream that God has placed in your heart? What are the obstacles to seeing that dream fulfilled? As you seek his will for your life, prayerfully ask for eyes of faith to help you see his will and his plan for you. Dare to ask great things of God, for he is a great God. Trust him to take your ability and your availability and use them mightily to impact your world for his glory. If you are passionate for Christ and willing to be used by him to effect positive change, then you can expect God to accomplish infinitely more than you might ask or think. Dare to believe and make a difference.

WHO TURNED
OFF THE LIGHT?

Do everything without complaining or arguing, so
that you may become blameless and pure, children
of God without fault in a crooked and depraved
generation, in which you shine like stars in the
universe as you hold out the word of life.

Philippians 2:14–16

Lately, my heart has been burdened about Christians, and
our role in bringing about the healing and change needed
in our society. I fear that we have become lukewarm in
our personal walk and that we are merely doing what is
needed to get by one day at a time. I wonder whether or
not those who observe us on a daily basis see anything in
us that sets us apart from the rest of our generation.

God calls us to do everything without complaining or arguing, yet how often do we do just the opposite? Whether it is complaining about our responsibilities on the job, our obligations at home, or our duty as tax-paying citizens in a society that continues to unravel at the seams, we are perhaps more prone to complain about all that is wrong rather than give thanks for what is right and good about our individual circumstances. Whatever happened to simply being thankful for the health to carry out God's calling, his daily provision regardless of where he has placed us to work, and the ability to stand and fight for his values? It all comes down to choice and attitude. We must choose to have a godly attitude and to work and serve one another without complaining.

When people look at us, do they see blameless and pure children of God who are without fault in a crooked and depraved generation? Sadly, I don't think so. Too many of us are guilty of compromising God's standards as set forth in his Word and living beneath the radar at times. We are guilty of backbiting, gossip, road rage, greed, and so many of the sins that plague our society.

For the most part, Christians probably don't live a whole lot differently than their non-Christian counterparts. Sure, we probably pray more (at least, I hope we do) and read our Bibles, but do we really live according to the Word of God, or are we "Sunday only" Christians? I believe there is no more powerful force in this world than a fully surrendered child of God who is willing to live a holy life grounded in the Word of God.

Our generation needs the truth and encouragement of Scripture. As God's children, we are called to shine like stars in the universe as we hold out the word of life. Are you shining like stars in your workplace, your home, and your community? Are you encouraging others with the words of God so that they may find strength to face each day and meet their challenges victoriously? Don't hide your light under a bushel. Let others see what God has done for you and is doing in you! You may be the only Jesus many people will see.

HIDE 'EM IN
YOUR HEART

And this is my prayer: that your love may abound
more and more in knowledge and depth of insight,
so that you may be able to discern what is best and
may be pure and blameless until the day of Christ.
                                          Philippians 1:9–10

One of my son's favorite children's videos was one by Steve
Green entitled "Hide 'Em in Your Heart." We watched
that video over and over and memorized every word to
every song. The theme of the video was based on Psalm
119:11: "I have hidden your word in my heart that I might
not sin against you."

One year, I didn't make the typical New Year's resolutions, but I did set a couple of goals to help me in my

walk with the Lord. The first goal was to read through the entire Bible. The second thing was to memorize Scripture, beginning with Philippians 1:9–10. I selected these verses because they reflect what God has laid on my heart—that we all need to be more knowledgeable of his truths, walk in love with one another, and strive to live blameless and pure lives before a watching world.

I challenge you to find one verse of Scripture today that brings you hope and encouragement and commit it to memory. You will find that hiding God's Word in your heart will give you the strength and courage you need to face your challenges, wisdom to make good decisions, and the discernment and determination to "conduct yourselves in a manner worthy of the gospel of Christ" (Philippians 1:27).

SECOND HELPINGS

Jesus answered, "It is written: Man does not live
on bread alone, but on every word that comes from
the mouth of God."

Matthew 4:4

God created our bodies with the unique ability to signal
us when they need food in order to properly function. I
know that if I don't eat breakfast, I will become irritable
and lethargic and lack the energy I need to get through a
busy morning.

Once, I attended a women's dinner meeting at church
and shared my healthy horse diet philosophy with the lady
sitting next to me: I am as healthy as a horse because I eat
like one. I eat heartily and try to make sure that I make
some healthy dietary choices every day. When I can, I eat
whatever it is I am craving because normally, that is the
only way my appetite is truly satisfied. However, I find

that eating what I want often creates a desire for more. It is the second helping that gets me into trouble.

While I try not to indulge in too many second helpings at mealtime, there is one food I can't get enough of—the Word of God. God's Word tells us, "Blessed are those who hunger and thirst for righteousness, for they will be filled" (Matthew 5:6). How can we know what righteousness is if we don't read about it in God's Word? How can we desire a more intimate relationship with Jesus if we don't come to know him through the pages of Scripture? How can we have peace and the assurance of God's provision, healing, faithfulness, love, and mercy if we don't open and read our Bibles daily?

I cherish my time in God's Word each morning. To start my day without it is to invite trouble into my life. I know I need the Sword of the Spirit to combat the enemy, to encourage me as I walk this journey every day, and to face my challenges with the knowledge that I am not alone. Without God's Word, I am a sitting duck for Satan, and he knows it. So are we all.

What are you feasting on today? It has been said that breakfast is the most important meal of the day, and physically speaking, that is true. But we are more than just physical bodies. We were created with a soul that needs the daily nourishment of God's Word to truly sustain us. And don't worry—it is the one food you can't eat too much of, so have a second helping!

I CAN ONLY IMAGINE

Then I heard a voice from heaven say, "Write:
Blessed are the dead who die in the Lord from
now on." "Yes," says the Spirit, "they will rest from
their labor, for their deeds will follow them."

Revelation 14:13

A few years ago, the contemporary Christian band,
MercyMe, released a song that became a hit not only on
Christian music charts, but on pop charts as well. "I Can
Only Imagine" captures the heart of our ultimate joy and
hope as Christians: spending eternity with Jesus and in
the company of loved ones who have preceded us in death.
As I mourn the recent deaths of two good friends, my
thoughts turn once more toward heaven and to those who
will be there to greet me on the day that Jesus calls me
home for good.

You don't have to look far to find people who are facing death. Both of my friends died of cancer, and many other friends are battling this horrible disease. Yet the friends who know Christ have the hope that God will heal them and the assurance that if he chooses not to, they will soon enter a glorious eternity in heaven, where there will be no more nausea from chemo, side effects from radiation, or the heartache of leaving loved ones behind. They know that something better awaits those who know Christ as Savior, and they are preparing themselves for the day that they will leave this earth for their heavenly home.

Yet there are those who will die without the blessed assurance that comes through salvation in Christ. If you know of someone who is facing death and an uncertain eternity, ask God to give you the opportunity and the boldness to share the gospel with them and to invite them to receive Christ. As long as they draw a breath, there is hope that they can be saved, but only if we are willing to share the reason for the hope that we have.

As you go about your day today, ask God to give you sensitivity toward those who are grieving the loss of a loved one or those who are facing the end of their earthly life. Pray for their peace, salvation, and comfort. Pray that God will make receptive the hearts of those who do not yet know him. Be the hands of God to those who need his touch so desperately. Their final hours may be your finest hour in terms of the ministry God has called you to. Fear not, for God is with you and will equip you to minister to those lost and hurting souls who need a Savior.

OUT OF THE FIRE

For who is God besides the LORD? And who is a
rock? Only our God. God—He clothes me with
strength and makes my way perfect.

Psalm 18:31–32, HCSB

Some days I question how perfect my way is. One day,
in particular, I was literally *in* the fire. While my daughter and her grandmother were baking cookies, the over-
filled cookie pans created a mess on the bottom of my
oven, which started a fire. I spent the entire day cooking
and cleaning up kitchen messes, doing laundry, and in
between, doing homework with my daughter. In the process, I had ample opportunity to learn a few things about
grace, patience, and unceasing prayer.

God was my strength that day. Without him, I know
I wouldn't have made it through the challenges of being
a patient hostess, firefighter, and homework helper. I

lost some battles and won others, but the day eventually ended, and I was able to once more rest in him.

We are all works in progress. God is refining us through every fiery trial we face. With each new day, we have a chance to start over and somehow live it a little better than the day before by acknowledging the Lord and praying for his grace and wisdom.

SAME OLD
STRUGGLES

.

He will call upon me, and I will answer him; I
will be with him in trouble, I will deliver him and
honor him.

Psalm 91:15

Don't you just feel sometimes that nothing in life changes?
It seems we deal with the same old struggles, never seeing
any real progress in the problem areas of life. When money
is tight and your back is up against the wall, it seems there is
always something that breaks or perhaps an unanticipated
medical expense that sabotages any effort on your part to
refrain from using credit cards or draining your savings
account to cover the shortfall. Frustrating, isn't it? We con-

stantly take three steps forward and two steps back, never quite reaching the light at the end of the tunnel.

Perhaps you just landed your dream job, only to find out you have a medical condition that will require you to take a leave of absence. What do you do then? How do you give thanks in all things when all you really want to say is, "God, why me? Why this? Why now?"

God is no stranger to the questions we ask. Certainly the Psalms are proof of that. David did not hold back from sharing his frustrations, fears, and disappointment with God because he knew he could boldly approach the Lord. He had that kind of relationship with God. Do you? Do you know that God loves you intimately and unconditionally and that he cares about every aspect of your life?

It is okay to ask the hard questions of God when life beats you up day in and day out. But will you stay tuned into him long enough to wait for his answers? Are you willing to hear what he has to say about your struggles and wait on him to provide the solution you need? I believe that in every struggle we face, God is right there, waiting to hear from us and to speak to us. God is all about relationship—his relationship with you.

If you are struggling with the same old issues of life, take a few minutes to quiet yourself before God, pour out your heart to him in prayer, and search his Word for the answers you need. You will find the answers if you seek and wait upon the Lord.

Dee Dee Wike

OPPOSITES ATTRACT

For those God foreknew he also predestined to be conformed to the likeness of his Son, that he might be the firstborn among many brothers. And those he predestined, he also called; those he called, he also justified; those he justified, he also glorified.

Romans 8:29–30

In 2007, my husband and I celebrated twenty years of marriage. How quickly those first two decades passed! When I met Steve, I'm not sure two people could have been more different. He was quiet, even-tempered, unassuming, and tightfisted when it came to money. I, on the other hand, was self-confident and moody, prone to spend freely, and looking for something more exciting from life than marriage to an accountant.

When I think back to the way we met, I know without a doubt that God ordained our relationship. Through the years we have been together, we have become a little more likeminded and have taken on some of each other's personality traits. Thankfully, Steve hasn't taken on my moodiness, but he has become more generous and less tightfisted. I have become a little more even-tempered (because of God's work in my life) and a little more conservative in my spending habits. We have both grown closer to the Lord through the years, and despite the road bumps we've hit along the way, love each other more today than the day we married.

Many of us have observed older couples who have begun to resemble each other as they have aged. That's the way Christ wants us to be as we mature in our relationship with him. We are to look more like him, exhibit more of his character than our own, and to be holy as he is holy. In short, we are to be conformed to his likeness, that his glory might be revealed in us.

Although we were created in God's image, we live in a world that does its best to conform us to its ideals by tempting us to sin and adhere to its values. Prone to wander far from grace, we look no different than our nonbelieving counterparts. Yet God sees us with tender and forgiving eyes. God will never compromise his character or standards, but he will always stand ready to receive, forgive, and transform a truly repentant sinner.

OPEN-BOOK TEST

Consider it all joy, my brothers, whenever you face trials of many kinds, because you know that the testing of your faith develops perseverance. Perseverance must finish its work so that you may be mature and complete, not lacking anything.

James 1:2–4

Our school day hadn't even started, and already I was dreading it. I was frustrated by my son's total lack of interest in school and the amount of time I had to spend adjusting to the computer-driven curriculum I had bought so that he might be a little more motivated to do his schoolwork. Nothing I tried seemed to help much. After a very hard week and an equally trying weekend, I went to bed that night not nearly prepared enough for the next day's tasks.

I am convinced that the real enemy of our homeschool was not my son's attention deficit and lack of interest but the devil himself. Two of Satan's most effective weapons against Christians are discouragement and distraction. Our only hope of persevering and passing the tests life gives us is to open the book that has all the answers and draw upon God's wisdom and grace to see us through our challenges. "The weapons we fight with are not the weapons of the world. On the contrary, they have divine power to demolish strongholds" (2 Corinthians 10:4). Satan may have established a foothold, but by the grace and power of God, it did not become a stronghold.

God alone knows the challenges we face and sees the outcome of these trials we are going through. He has a reason for everything and is working all things together for our good (Romans 8:28). Ask him for the strength to persevere in your trials and to use you to encourage others who may be facing challenges of their own.

Satan's wiles are no match for the weapons of God's Word and prayer. Put on the full armor of God so that you will be able to withstand every flaming arrow of discouragement and distraction the enemy has in his quiver. Fight with confidence knowing the battle belongs to the Lord.

Dee Dee Wike

DREAMS REALLY DO COME TRUE

Delight yourself in the LORD and he will give you
the desires of your heart.

Psalm 37:4

After years of writing journals and dreaming that one
day my writings might actually be published, my dream
finally came true. One cold February morning, I received
the happy news that my manuscript had been accepted for
publication and that the contract for my first book was in
the works. How I looked forward to the day when I would
actually hold a copy of that first book in my hand.

All praise and glory belong to the one who gave me
the dream and made it a reality. He is the great author,
having written my favorite book of all time, the Bible. His

words have inspired my own and have given me the courage to even dare to dream of becoming a published author. Once more he has proven that he is faithful to his Word, that his promises can be trusted, and that he is the giver of our hearts' desires.

So many times through the years, God has heard my prayers and fulfilled my dreams of being happily married, a stay-at-home mom, and his servant. He has allowed me to discover and use my gifts for his glory, to encourage others, and to make a difference. I am humbled, so humbled that he would answer my prayers in this way.

Never think that God can't use you, or that you don't have gifts to offer him. Never give up on your dreams. If God has placed a dream in your heart, a desire that fuels your passion, delight yourself in Him, pray it through, and never stop believing that it can come true.

A dream that will need all the love you can give
Everyday of your life, for as long as you live
Climb every mountain, ford every stream
Follow every rainbow, till you find your dream
—Oscar Hammerstein II

Dee Dee Wike

HOPE IS REAL

Why are you downcast, O my soul? Why so disturbed within me? Put your hope in God, for I will yet praise him, my Savior and my God.

Psalm 42:11

In 2010, I lost a friend to cancer. One afternoon, I sat beside the heap of flowers piled on her grave and wept. I asked God, "Why? Why Nancy? Why cancer? Why couldn't you have taken a murderer instead, or at least kept her from suffering so much?" Those are questions for which I'll never have an answer. God is God. He is merciful and loving, but he is also sovereign. I don't have to have answers. I only have to know that *he is*.

On my drive to the cemetery, the MercyMe song "I Can Only Imagine" was playing on the radio. Thoughts turned toward my friend, who now knows what I can only imagine, that heaven is real and being in the presence of

Jesus far outweighs any suffering she experienced on earth. Interestingly, Matthew West's song "Save a Place for Me" was playing as I drove home, a reminder that Nancy, along with other friends and family who have gone before me, is saving a place for me in heaven. She is not hurting any longer. Nancy has been completely healed in every way for all eternity.

God's Word gives us real hope, not just for those we love who are perishing, but for those of us who remain to carry on the battle for men's souls. Those of us who have received Christ as our Savior through the miracle of reconciliation have been made righteous through him and have the hope of spending the rest of our lives—both in heaven and on earth—in his presence. We have been given the ministry of reconciliation (2 Corinthians 5:18) so that we can share with others the reason for the hope that we have (1 Peter 3:15).

If you are feeling hopeless today, then "I pray also that the eyes of your heart may be enlightened in order that you may know the hope to which he has called you, the riches of his glorious inheritance in the saints, and his incomparably great power for us who believe" (Ephesians 1:18–19).

BELIEVING
IS SEEING

Then Jesus said to the centurion, "Go! It will be done just as you believed it would." And his servant was healed that very hour.

Matthew 8:13

For so long, many of us have heard and perhaps even said the phrase, "I'll believe it when I see it." The problem with that point of view, particularly when it comes to faith in God, is that we feel we must see God's hand at work in our lives before we believe that he even exists or will do what he has promised he will do.

Despite all the signs and wonders that God performed in the days leading up to the exodus of the Israelites, many still doubted his ability to deliver them from Egypt and from the hand of Pharaoh. When they were on the shore of the Red Sea with nowhere to run from Pharaoh's army, they cried out to God in fear and complained to Moses for bringing them to the desert to die. Once more, God proved himself mighty by parting the sea and taking them through on dry ground, drowning all the soldiers in pursuit of them. "And when the Israelites *saw* the great power the LORD displayed against the Egyptians, the people feared the LORD and put their trust in him and in Moses his servant" (Exodus 14:31). Do you wonder why they had to repeatedly see God's signs and wonders before they could fear and trust the Lord? Are we not the same?

Contrast the Israelites and the majority of us with the centurion in Matthew chapter eight. Here is a man who approached Jesus to ask healing for his servant. When Jesus offered to go to the centurion's house to heal his servant, the centurion replied, "Lord, I do not deserve to have you come under my roof. But just say the word, and my servant will be healed" (vs. 8). Not only did the centurion display great faith but humility as well. He knew his place and the power of Jesus's words. He needed no proof of Christ's ability to heal.

Why is it we need proof that God is who he says he is and that he can do what he has promised in his Word? In these times of economic uncertainty, I stand strongly on God's promises of provision for my family. The future of my husband's job in the banking industry is uncertain, but of this I am sure: God has promised to supply all our needs according to his riches in glory in Christ Jesus (Philippians 4:19). He promises to give us everything we need for life—one day at a time—if we will seek first the

Dee Dee Wike

Lord and his righteousness (Matthew 6:33). I need not worry about tomorrow (v. 34), for I know that God holds me in his hand and that he has a good plan for me—a plan to prosper and not harm me (Jeremiah 29:11).

What are you holding on to? The hope that tomorrow you will still have a job, or the promise of God that he will provide for you? Do you have to see money in the bank to know that your needs will be supplied, or do you trust in God to fulfill his promises in your behalf?

Today, try living with the "believing is seeing" philosophy. Believe in God *first* and *see* what good things he has in store for you.

STUBBORN STAINS

…and to present her to himself as a radiant church,
without stain or wrinkle or any other blemish.

Ephesians 5:27

My daughter and I had the privilege of being selected as product testers for a laundry product that promised to block stains before they ever had a chance of setting into our clothes. When the crew from our local news station came to our house to film the station's weekly "Does It Work?" segment, we laundered and treated items with the product then proceeded to stain the garments with coffee, punch, spaghetti sauce, and Italian salad dressing to see if the product did what it advertised. The end result was that some of the stains set in, ruining the clean white tee shirt we used for the test.

Sin is like that. It has a way of marring our lives and leaving stains that make us feel dirty on the inside and

Dee Dee Wike

ugly on the outside. Because of our fallen nature, every one of us is prone to sin at one time or another. There is no stain repellent that can keep us from being tainted by sin, but knowing God's Word certainly helps us discern and avoid sin if we read and obey it.

While we may not escape sin, we can be cleansed from it and washed "whiter than snow" (Psalm 51:7). The blood of Jesus, shed for us on Calvary, not only cleanses and washes away our sin but also makes us righteous in the eyes of God.

> This righteousness from God comes through faith in Jesus Christ to all who believe. There is no difference, for all have sinned and fall short of the glory of God, and are justified freely by his grace through the redemption that came by Jesus Christ.
>
> Romans 3:22–24

Is there some sin in your life that makes you feel unclean? If you confess your sin, accept Jesus as your Savior, and receive his free gift of salvation, then what he has said will be true of you: "Blessed are those who wash their robes, that they may have the right to the tree of life and may go through the gates into the city" (Revelation 22:14).

NO GREATER LOVE

Greater love has no one than this, that he lay down his life for his friends.

John 15:13

On Valentine's Day, we celebrate our love for others by buying cards, gifts, and candy. We acknowledge those who mean the most to us and hope that, in turn, we are acknowledged by others.

Jesus spoke often about love and embodied love in ways that no other man or woman ever has. He taught us that love is selfless, serving, and sacrificial, but how well do we really understand the true nature of love?

In teaching about selfless love, the apostle Paul said, "Do nothing out of selfish ambition or vain conceit, but in humility consider others better than yourselves. Each of you should look not only to your own interests, but also to the interests of others" (Philippians 2:3–4). In our society, we are taught just the opposite—to "look out for number one" and take care of ourselves first. We have become the center of our own universe, often neglecting the needs and wants of those around us.

In the same passage, we are also taught that ours should be a serving love.

> Your attitude should be the same as that of Christ Jesus: Who, being in very nature God, did not consider equality with God something to be grasped, but made himself nothing, taking the very nature of a servant, being made in human likeness.
>
> Philippians 2:5–7

Jesus was not above serving others. From his willingness to stop and heal those who came across his path to washing the feet of his disciples, Jesus served.

But Jesus also taught us about the greatest kind of love: sacrificial love. He, who committed no sin (1 Peter 2:22), laid down his life as the atoning sacrifice for our sins, past, present, and future. Yet we complain about having to sacrifice anything—time, money, convenience—to serve him by serving those he brings into our lives.

What the world needs now is not love, sweet love. Rather this world needs love that is selfless, serving, and sacrificial. When you celebrate Valentine's Day, pray that God will give you his eyes to see the needs of others and his heart to love others as he would.

LIFE IS NOT A POPULARITY CONTEST

Blessed are you when people insult you, persecute you and falsely say all kinds of evil against you because of me. Rejoice and be glad, because great is your reward in heaven, for in the same way they persecuted the prophets who were before you.

Matthew 5:11–12

For the brief period that I homeschooled my children, I occasionally received critical remarks from both people I know and people who were total strangers to me. Odds are you, too, have been in a situation where others said things about you that were hurtful, or at the least, confusing. In those circumstances, what did you do? Did you buckle under the criticism, or did you let the negative comments roll off your back like water off a duck?

Being a Christian in today's world is not an easy task. Choosing to stand for God's causes is unpopular and puts us at risk of being persecuted or ridiculed for our beliefs and our lifestyle. The same can be said of parenting. I had to remind my teenage son last night that I am his mother, not his friend, and that as a parent, I am not in a popularity contest. I will do what I think is in his best interest, whether or not he likes it or thinks it is fair.

If we are walking with Christ, living in obedience to his Word, and standing for his causes in this world, we will have tribulation. Even the blessed and faithful ones will not be exempt from suffering and hardship. That includes you and me. "For it has been granted to you on behalf of Christ not only to believe on him, but also to suffer for him" (Philippians 1:29).

To those of you who are the recipient of someone else's criticism, I offer you these words of encouragement to persevere in the good that you do for the sake of Christ and the gospel: "But rejoice that you participate in the sufferings of Christ, so that you may be overjoyed when his glory is revealed. If you are insulted because of the name of Christ, you are blessed, for the Spirit of glory and of God rests on you" (1 Peter 4:14–15).

JOY AFTER THE MOURNING

Those who sow in tears will reap with songs of joy.
Psalm 126:5

Contrary to what many believe, I really don't have my act together. I have bad days, same as anybody else, but usually in the midst of my difficulties, I can find some reason to be joyful. Not happy, necessarily, but certainly joyful.

There was a time not long ago that was especially difficult as I was forced to play my "parent" card and discipline my children. Anytime I find myself in a place of conflict with my kids, I feel intense sorrow. I would rather be a friend than a parent any day, but some days I am required to be a parent, enforcing rules and teaching character.

But God gently reminds me of the responsibility I have to teach my children his ways and of the joy that will be mine when the seeds of love I have sown have yielded a harvest of righteousness in their lives. When I recall his mercy and grace in my life, God restores the hope that my children will one day also receive his mercy and grow in his grace.

I have shed many tears as a parent—tears of frustration, disappointment, and sorrow. I have said things in anger that I wish I could take back, and things in love that were hard for me to say. Surely God knows what that is like. We are all his children and some of us get a little wayward at times. His Word is full of hard sayings, and at the same time, loving compassion and mercy. What better example of a parent could we follow than that of our heavenly Father?

One of the most stirring images from Mel Gibson's movie *The Passion of the Christ* was the teardrop, presumably God's, which fell from heaven when Christ died on the cross. I have no doubt that God has shed many a tear because of his great love and concern for us. If God was not spared heartbreak, why should we expect to be?

During times like this, I hold on to the promise of God that "his anger lasts only a moment, but his favor lasts a lifetime; weeping may remain for a night, but rejoicing comes in the morning" (Psalm 30:5).

Your season of sorrow may seem endless, but God's promise is true. If you're his child, cry out to your heavenly Father. He is there, he is listening, and he will restore your joy as you place your trust in him.

DO YOUR BEST

Do your best to present yourself to God as one approved, a workman who does not need to be ashamed and who correctly handles the word of truth.

2 Timothy 2:15

"Do your best" is a phrase we hear often but a practice many of us fail to execute with consistency. It is something I encourage my children to do but am often guilty of failing to do in many areas of my own life: housekeeping, financial management, loving my spouse, teaching my children—the list goes on. Rather than push myself to do everything with excellence, I settle for second best more often than I care to admit. Probably most of us do. God deserves better than that from us, doesn't he?

I believe that if we truly worked to serve God's purposes and to look to him alone for approval, we would set higher standards for our behavior and do our best with a little

Dee Dee Wike

more consistency. For instance, my husband is very tolerant when it comes to my housekeeping. He understands that I have more to do than clean, cook, and do laundry. I often stop short of doing what I should do because I don't approach housekeeping with God's approval in mind. If I did, then my housekeeping would reflect it.

There are many areas of our lives in which we may fall short of God's standards and which don't reflect a conscious effort to honor the Lord. One area, though, where we can strive to do our best is correctly handling the word of truth, God's Word, as we read it and use it to encourage others. If we don't live in total obedience to it, though, how effective can we truly be in holding out the Word of life to those who need it most?

Thankfully, God is patient. I am a work in progress, and God is not finished with me yet. Neither is he finished with you. Because of his great mercy and grace, we have the blessed hope that each day will bring new opportunities to do our best to honor him in all we do.

BETWEEN A ROCK
AND A HARD PLACE

The LORD is my rock, my fortress and my deliverer;
my God is my rock, in whom I take refuge.

Psalm 18:2

Lately, I have found myself in a very hard place involving a family matter. It has made every aspect of my life—school, work, and our everyday routine—more stressful and challenging. Because of the nature of the problem, my emotions have ranged from anger and hurt to utter frustration at times, and dealing with the problem has left me utterly exhausted.

Well-meaning individuals have offered both kind advice and harsh criticism as we have sought solutions from those who have already been down this road.

Responses have been quite revealing in terms of possible remedies and human nature itself. I have learned a great deal just from the responses I have received and pray that if ever my advice is sought on a similar matter, my reply will be a kind but truthful one to the person who finds herself in my shoes.

How thankful I am for God's assurances that "our light and momentary troubles are achieving for us an eternal glory that far outweighs them all" (2 Corinthians 4:17) and "My grace is sufficient for you, for my power is made perfect in weakness" (2 Corinthians 12:9). I know that Jesus, my rock, is in this hard place with me, comforting and teaching me so that I can, in turn, help someone else through a similar challenge some day (2 Corinthians 1:3–4).

As difficult as this journey has been, God is using it for my good. He is supplying the grace, love, and strength I need each day to stand in the hard place so that others may see and believe in the one who is our ever-present help in time of need (Psalm 46:1).

THIS ONE'S FOR ME

What, then, shall we say in response to this? If
God is for us, who can be against us?

Romans 8:31

Raising a teenage son was difficult at times. Once the rag-
ing hormones of adolescence kicked in, the adjustment
to his challenging behavior became trying for all of us.
When his schoolwork began to suffer, we tried motivating
him by removing or restricting certain privileges. Most
days, though, we just suffered and prayed our way through
this challenging season of life.

The difficulties of life keep me on my knees most days,
praying for a more Spirit-controlled response to all that
takes place around me. As hard as our challenges may
seem at times, it is through our trials that we grow and
learn patience and perseverance (James 1:2–4). It is in our

difficulties that we learn to seek God's wisdom (v. 5) and direction for the perplexing issues of life.

I believe that a lot of what we experienced with our son was a manifestation of the spiritual warfare we encounter every day as Christians. Let's face it—Satan will do anything to hinder the spread of the gospel, especially when we are growing and moving in God's direction. If Satan cannot distract us with irritating problems, he will use them to discourage us. Our weapons in this fight are prayer and the promises of Scripture that God is for us. Nothing Satan attempts to do can overshadow God's purpose and plan for our lives.

If the deck is seemingly stacked against you, know this: God trumps Satan every time. The battle has been won. That's not to say that you don't have to fall on your knees and pray your way through the battle. Satan doesn't give up easily, nor should we.

"You, dear children, are from God and have overcome them, because the one who is in you is greater than the one who is in the world" (1 John 4:4).

IT'S NOT A SMALL WORLD AFTER ALL

Therefore go and make disciples of all nations, baptizing them in the name of the Father and of the Son and of the Holy Spirit, and teaching them to obey everything I have commanded you. And surely I will be with you always, to the very end of the age.

Matthew 28:19–20

As my kids and I prepared for a visit to the Magic Kingdom at Disneyworld, I couldn't get the song "It's A Small World" out of my mind. With each passing day and every friend added to my Facebook, I realize that nothing could be further from the truth. My world isn't small. On the contrary, it is constantly growing.

Hardly a day goes by that I don't thank God for the Internet. I am not sure how I ever functioned without it.

Dee Dee Wike

Because of technology, we not only have access to a vast array of information but also the ability to communicate with millions of people all over the world. In a sense, the world has become our virtual neighborhood.

Jesus instructed his disciples to take the gospel to the ends of the earth, and thankfully, we have men and women called by God who serve as foreign missionaries around the world. While you or I may not be called to serve on foreign soil, we are called to be missionaries where we work, live, and play. He has given us tremendous tools and opportunities to share his message with the world around us.

My mission field right now includes writing inspirational non-fiction for those who are seeking a new or deeper relationship with Jesus. I am using my gifts to promote the cause of Christ when and where I can. God has given each of us gifts and called us to make him known throughout the world, no matter how large or small our circle of influence might be.

Have you figured out what your gift is or how to use it to share the love of Jesus with those around you? Ask God, and he will show you how you can reach your world for Christ and for his glory.

SACRIFICE OR SERVICE?

For God did not call us to be impure, but to live a holy life.

> 1 Thessalonians 4:7

Ash Wednesday marks the beginning of the Lenten season on the Christian calendar. Commonly observed in more liturgical denominations, it is a solemn day of repentance for Christians the world over and marks the beginning of the days leading up to Easter. In the Episcopal Church where I grew up, we observed this holy day by attending a worship service and having ashes placed on our foreheads in the sign of the cross to signify repentance from our sins. Accompanying that tradition was the practice of fasting or abstaining from something that gave us pleasure. As a child, it was my practice to give up candy or soft drinks. We lived for Sunday, our weekly feast day, and particularly Easter Sunday, the day when our season of penitence ended.

I am no longer a member of the Episcopal Church, but I still observe Lent in my own way. Some years, I actually do give up something I enjoy. One year, I gave up coffee because it is my favorite beverage. That, however, proved to be a mistake as I suffered from the headaches of caffeine withdrawal. Other years, I have opted not to sacrifice temporal indulgences but rather to sacrifice time in order to serve others and grow deeper in my relationship with the Lord.

If you were to choose a way to observe Lent, remember the sacrifice of our Lord and consider his season of fasting, how would you do it? Would you give up something that brings you pleasure, or would you commit yourself to serve others as he would have you do? I think the important thing for all of us is to take a step back, truly consider what he endured as he walked this earth, and consider the price he paid for our sins. In following his example of sacrifice and service, we would be doing something to bring him pleasure and glory.

THE LIST MAKER

In his heart a man plans his course; but the LORD
determines his steps.

Proverbs 16:9

On my journey through the Old Testament, I have been
amazed at the amount of detail God gave his people
regarding so much of life. From the way the ark was
constructed to every aspect of the tabernacle's construc-
tion and every article to be used or placed inside it, God
provided intricate details. I have been especially amazed
by the precise instructions given in the book of Leviticus
regarding sacrificial offerings. Who but God would have
the mind to retain all that information? How fearful
might Moses and Aaron have been that they would leave
out some detail and totally mess things up?

Many of us are list makers. I sometimes think that is
one reason why we experience so much stress in our daily

Dee Dee Wike

lives. We feel compelled to accomplish everything on our lists, keep every appointment on our calendars, and make sure that everything is done decently and in order.

As I was having my prayer time this morning, I wrote the following words in my journal:

> I wish I could just clear my calendar and do nothing but soak up your presence and your Word and bask in your peace. Life won't let me. I have a full day indeed, and that's just for starters.

While I continued to pray about everything on my list that I needed to accomplish, God impressed upon my spirit that he already knows. He knows the beginning and the end of all that concerns me for he is the Alpha and Omega, the Beginning and the End (Revelation 21:6). I can rest in the fact that God knows the details of all that concerns me and is working in my behalf to see everything accomplished in his perfect timing.

God is very good at what he does. I need only to look through the pages of Scripture to see how perfectly he works things out.

I will continue making my lists, but no longer will I be ruled by them. I will commit to the Lord whatever I do, knowing that my plans will succeed and that he will work out everything for his own ends (Proverbs 16:3–4).

THE POWER OF CANCELLATION

God made him who had no sin to be sin for us, so that in him we might become the righteousness of God.

2 Corinthians 5:21

Life has a way of altering my schedule from time to time and requiring me to rethink and adjust the plans I have made. A sick child or one appointment too many on an overloaded calendar is all the motivation I need to cancel everything for a day. If I am smart enough to make the adjustment, I can know that God has something even better in store for me, like a little rest, or better yet, a few extra minutes with him.

Few things make me feel more empowered than cancelling my appointments for the day. When I realize that God, not my calendar, is the one calling the shots, it becomes easy to skip that event I have planned for weeks to attend or my kids' weekly allergy shots (not a life or death medical appointment) without feeling guilt or regret.

Jesus knows the power of cancellation. His death on the cross cancelled the very sin that separated mankind from an eternity with him. He wasn't obligated to die for our sins; he willingly chose to give up his very life because of his great love for humanity and a desire to fellowship with us. His love was all the motivation he needed to cancel our sin debt on the cross in order to have us all to himself.

The next time you need to cancel an appointment or receive a cancellation notice, don't consider it an inconvenience. Rather, let it serve as a reminder to you of the high price Jesus paid to cancel your sin debt just because he wanted to spend eternity with you. Take a few minutes today to tell him how much you appreciate him for laying aside everything, even his very life, to secure your salvation and claim you as his own.

GIVE IT ALL YOU'VE GOT

We have different gifts, according to the grace given us. If a man's gift is prophesying, let him use it in proportion to his faith. If it is serving, let him serve; if it is teaching, let him teach; if it is encouraging, let him encourage; if it is contributing to the needs of others, let him give generously; if it is leadership, let him govern diligently; if it is showing mercy, let him do it cheerfully.

Romans 12:6–8

Do you ever wish that you could do something really significant? Something that really makes a difference in someone's life? One of the greatest joys in life is discovering your God-given talents and using them to serve those in need. Each of us requires help from time to time, and each of us has gifts that we can share with others. The question is, do we? Or are we so caught up in our own problems that we ignore the needs of others and keep our gifts to ourselves?

Recently, I had the opportunity to serve a hurting friend who had a very big need. She didn't even have to ask—I was compelled to help, driven, almost. Yet I knew I couldn't do all she needed on my own. I needed others to come alongside me with their gifts and insights. Most of all, I needed God to orchestrate everything, and he did. With his help and the help of a few friends, I was able to do my part to meet her need.

When is the last time you offered your gifts to God to be used by him to make a difference in someone else's life? If you look around, you will see plenty of opportunities to serve others. The funny thing is, once you give of yourself and your talents to meet the needs of others, you will find yourself on the receiving end of a whole lot of joy.

A MOST
EXCELLENT REST

Come to me, all you who are weary and burdened,
and I will give you rest. Take my yoke upon you
and learn from me, for I am gentle and humble in
heart, and you will find rest for your souls. For my
yoke is easy and my burden is light.

Matthew 11:28–30

I love naps, especially the kind where you get so relaxed that
you drool on the pillowcase. That's gross, I realize, but a
little drool is always evidence that my nap was truly restful.

Recently, I found myself in an exhausting race against
the elements—the threat of losing electricity to falling
tree limbs during an ice storm (what an eerie sound that
is) and the clock, as I worked feverishly to clean house
and bake cookies so my teenager could entertain friends

on a rare snow day. While the kids slept in, I was at Wal-Mart picking up a few more groceries to carry us through the weekend, just in case the roads didn't clear quickly. By early afternoon, I was exhausted and ready for a well-deserved nap.

We spend so much of our time moving from one activity to the next that we don't often allow time for the rest our bodies and minds need. We over schedule ourselves, taking on too many commitments and not allowing for those precious quiet moments to reflect on God's goodness, seek his direction, and refresh ourselves with the spiritual nutrition and encouragement of his Word. Eventually, we collapse under the weight of the burdens we carry and burn out from too much activity and stress.

Jesus invites us to come into his presence and find rest for our weary souls and bodies. God himself ordained that we should rest from our labors when he rested from his own (Genesis 2:2–3). If God, who created all that we see, saw fit to take a little time off, so can we.

If you are physically tired and emotionally depleted, perhaps a nap or a good night's sleep is just what you need. As you lay your head on the pillow tonight and pull the covers up around your neck, close your eyes, take a deep relaxing breath, and thank God for his blessings in your life.

LITTLE ICE CUBE
WITH WHEELS

Give thanks in all circumstances, for this is God's
will for you in Christ Jesus.

1 Thessalonians 5:18

Yesterday, we found ourselves on the receiving end of
nature's glory (or wrath depending on your point of view)
as a major winter storm plowed through the area dumping
a little snow and just enough ice to make things interesting and a little inconvenient. Although not as devastating locally as the 1994 ice storm, this one still resulted in
power outages, hazardous travel, and quite a bit of damage to the trees in the neighborhood. I was thankful that
the only apparent damage we sustained was to a gutter on
the front of our house. Even though the streets were driv-
able, I was thankful I didn't have to go anywhere. My little

ice cube with wheels could stay parked in the driveway, at least for one more day.

When the lights went out at 9:45 p.m., the kids and I watched a short video on my battery-powered laptop before going to bed. I was thankful for my laptop and the time my kids and I enjoyed snuggling together. The house was delightfully quiet for a while, and after the movie, I drifted off into a restful slumber, only to be jolted awake by the sound of tree limbs falling on the roof above my head. I moved to a quieter room, the den, where the wall clock seemed to tick more loudly than normal. I was thankful for battery-powered clocks and flashlights during a power outage.

Despite the loud tick tock, I was able to drift back off to sleep. The silence of the night was broken by the *beep, beep* of the alarm system, alerting me of a power outage, as if I didn't already know. A 2:30 a.m. call to the alarm company yielded the information I needed to silence the incessant, high-pitched beeping. I was thankful that we didn't lose our telephone service and that the alarm company was staffed at that time of night.

About the time I drifted back to sleep, the lights suddenly popped on, and the electronic equipment began to whir and hum as power was restored shortly after 3:00 a.m. I was definitely thankful for the heat to kick back on as the temperature inside my home had dropped to forty-nine degrees! Despite all the sleep disturbances, I felt a deep sense of gratitude to God, who watched over us and wrapped us in his blanket of love.

WRITTEN DOWN

Jesus did many other miraculous signs in the presence of his disciples, which are not recorded in this book. But these are written that you may believe that Jesus is the Christ, the Son of God, and that by believing you may have life in his name.

John 20:30–31

This past Christmas, I purchased a new laptop to replace an older model, which no longer worked. Always looking for a more efficient way to do things, I began journaling on my new computer instead of writing out my journal entries by hand. Past experience has taught me that technology has its place and that some things are better done the old-fashioned way. Journaling is no exception. Somehow introducing technology into my quiet-time routine detracted from the intimacy of my precious

Dee Dee Wike

moments with the Lord, so I decided to resume the practice of writing my journal entries by hand.

Once I pen my thoughts in ink, they are written down for good. Computers crash, and files are lost, but what is written in ink can last a lifetime. God's Word was written down for all of us to read that we might believe in Jesus and find the strength, truth, and resources we need for daily living. Just as my journals will remain behind long after I am gone or my computer finds its final resting place in the landfill, God's Word will endure for all eternity. Jesus said, "Heaven and earth will pass away, but my words will never pass away" (Matthew 24:35). My journals will serve as a testimony of God's faithfulness and a reminder to those who follow me that God's Word is something we can depend on in every circumstance of life.

If you want to live a life of joy and purpose, pick up and read the Bible, God's written Word. It is his love letter to you. Even though the Bible was penned thousands of years ago, its truths are relevant and applicable to modern-day life. Technology will continue to change, but God's love and his truths never will. After you have spent a few minutes reading what God has written to you, pick up a pen and write a love letter back to him in your own journal. Write down the message he impresses upon your heart. Make it personal. After all, he who created you is intimately acquainted with all your ways (Psalm 139:3), and he longs to be gracious to you (Isaiah 30:18).

RUNNING CONVERSATION

Pray continually.

1 Thessalonians 5:17

We all know people who can talk a thing to death, don't we? Perhaps you are one of those people who can carry on a conversation with a signpost. I personally know people like that, and it is all I can do sometimes not to plug my ears or pull my hair out. I have become good at simply hitting the virtual "mute" button or simply tuning them out. Guess that makes me a bad listener, or worse, a bad friend.

A good friend will listen to you pour your heart out, no many how many times you have said the same thing. He also knows how to speak the truth in love (Ephesians 4:15) and will encourage you to be still and not fret (Psalm 37:7) about the things that are troubling you. A good friend is full of grace, love, patience, and wisdom. You know your deepest secrets are safe with him and that he will never betray your trust. He will not condemn you for anything you say or do. His love is constant and unconditional. As much as I love my closest friends on this earth, there is only one friend who embodies all these characteristics, Jesus.

Perhaps you think that Jesus is somewhere over the rainbow or off in the wild blue yonder, but he's actually much closer than that. He is as close as your next breath, and he invites you into an intimate relationship with him—the kind of relationship that lends itself to a running conversation with him wherever you go. In fact, we are commanded in Scripture to "pray continually." Prayer is both the act of speaking and the practice of listening to God, and we have the opportunity to do that twenty-four-seven. God is always online, never out of town, and never, ever too busy to listen to you. Even though he is the sovereign Almighty God, he cares about every aspect of your life, large and small. He has given you his written Word, the Bible, to guide, instruct, and encourage you on your journey through life. His greatest desire is for you to know and delight in him, even as he knows (Psalm 139), delights in, and rejoices over you with singing (Zephaniah 3:17).

If you dare to believe that God is real and that he sent his Son, Jesus, to bridge the gap between you and him, then you can have the kind of relationship with him that I do. Simply confess your sins and ask Jesus to live in your heart, and the way will be opened for an intimate relationship with him. There is no greater joy in life than knowing my God will always be there for me and that he will never forsake or betray me (Joshua 1:5). He can't because he is God.

WHERE'S THE IBUPROFEN?

Go up to the land flowing with milk and honey. But I will not go with you, because you are a stiff-necked people and I might destroy you on the way. When the people heard these distressing words, they began to mourn and no one put on any ornaments. For the LORD had said to Moses, "Tell the Israelites, 'You are a stiff-necked people. If I were to go with you even for a moment, I might destroy you.'"

Exodus 33:3–5

Yesterday, I sent my husband into the attic to retrieve some homeschool materials I was planning to sell. In the process of handing down a rather heavy box of books, he lost his grip, and for a moment I was transported back to the day when we were cutting a limb out of a tree following a storm. In my first book, Good to the Last Drop: Refreshing Inspiration for Homeschool Moms and Other Busy Women, I told the story of how being hardheaded saved my life one particular day. However, it was my stiff neck that saved me from the falling box of books and has me now asking, where's the ibuprofen?

Being stiff-necked can be a good thing when your husband loses his grip and you happen to be in the way; however, it is not a quality that God likes in his children. As today's Scripture reading shows, God rebuked the Israelites for being stiff-necked and told them that he would not accompany them into the land of milk and honey because he might just destroy them. While being stiff-necked may have prevented a greater injury to me, it could well have resulted in God's destruction of the Israelites.

A great many Christians are stiff-necked these days. Carnal Christians, as they are commonly called, are more interested in their own agendas than in God's, and they are determined to carry out the desires of their sinful flesh rather than walk in the fruit of the Spirit, surrendered to God's will. The Bible has a warning for these stiff-necked believers: "A man who remains stiff-necked after many rebukes will suddenly be destroyed—without remedy" (Proverbs 29:1).

How is your neck today? Is it sore from being stiff so long? Rather than reach for the ibuprofen, why not open and read God's Word and seek his forgiveness? The grace you find in scripture will prove to be the best medicine for what ails you. "He will not always accuse, nor will he harbor his anger forever; he does not treat us as our sins deserve or repay us according to our iniquities...as far as the east is from the west, so far has he removed our transgressions from us" (Psalm 103:9–12).

Don't let your sin separate you from God any longer. He loves you and longs to be with you everywhere you go.

GUINEA PIGS
ON SKATES

There are different kinds of gifts, but the same
Spirit. There are different kinds of service, but the
same Lord. There are different kinds of working,
but the same God works all of them in all men.
Now to each one the manifestation of the Spirit is
given for the common good.

1 Corinthians 12:4–7

During the Winter Olympics, I had been hard at work on
a writing project and missed most of the sporting events.
Among my favorite events to watch is figure skating. It is
such an elegant sport. When I posted a Facebook status
update stating I was taking a short break to clean out the
guinea pig's cage and watch a little of the pairs competition,
a friend posted the following comment: "When you really
need a break is if you ever think you just saw the guinea pig

ice skating!" Personally, I think my little guinea pig would look cute in a spandex costume and a tiny pair of skates.

Being an ice skater was always something I thought I might like to do, but that wasn't God's plan for me. We can't all be champion figure skaters. But God has given each of us has a special gift of great value to this world, one to use for his fame and glory, not our own. Do you know what your special gift is? What is that one thing you do perhaps better than anyone else that is making an impact on the world around you? If you aren't sure what your gift is, ask God to reveal it to you. There is nothing more fulfilling than using your God-given talents and abilities to serve him and minister to the people he places in your path each day.

Whatever your gift is, use it to honor God, and he will, in turn, honor you. Perhaps not with an Olympic medal or a best-selling book but a crown that will last forever (1 Corinthians 9:25) and the joy of knowing that you are making a positive difference in the lives of the people around you for his glory.

THE GREAT RACE

His divine power has given us everything we need
for life and godliness through our knowledge of
him who called us by his own glory and goodness.

2 Peter 1:3

A few years ago while visiting my husband's parents in
east Tennessee, we were privileged to go to the Bristol
Motor Speedway to enjoy the drive-thru Christmas light
display. It was an experience I shall never forget and one
of the highlights of that particular visit. No stranger
to extravagant holiday light exhibits, I expected to see
brightly colored lights in all manner of festive display, but
never in my wildest dreams could I have imagined driving on the racetrack where so many legends have raced.
Granted, we were only driving fifteen miles per hour. But
still, I delighted—and still do to this day—in telling some

of my male relatives and friends, especially the NASCAR fans, that I had driven on the track at Bristol.

Last spring, I took my kids to Disneyworld, and we visited the Test Track attraction at Epcot. I learned a lot that day as our car was put through test after test in all manner of road conditions and temperature extremes. Our test ride culminated with a thrilling sixty-mile-per-hour run around an oval track in a sporty convertible race-car. It was perhaps the closest thing to NASCAR I will ever experience.

Every day, we run a race. The road conditions vary from day to day and season to season. Have we equipped our-selves to run the race in such a way that we will win? Who is coaching us in our quest for the prize? Those of us who have a personal relationship with Jesus can answer those questions easily. "His divine power has given us everything we need for life and godliness through our knowledge of him who called us by his own glory and goodness" (2 Peter 1:3, NIV). His Word, the Bible, is our road map for the jour-ney, pointing us to the finish line and telling us all we need to know in order to finish the race well.

Whether we are in the slow lane or the fast lane, we are all moving toward a finish line that will mark the end of our race on this earth. When we reach the end of our journey, who will be waiting for us at the finish line? If Jesus is in the driver's seat because we accepted his free gift of salvation during our life on earth, then God him-self will be waiting to welcome us to his winner's circle—heaven. Those who have not received Jesus as Savior will

Dee Dee Wike

be disqualified and make an eternal pit stop in hell, forever separated from God, his love, and his light.

Are you prepared to cross the finish line and take your place in the winner's circle? Have you run the race in such a way as to claim the prize of eternal life? If not, then take a few minutes to talk to your coach and set things right once and for all by confessing your sin, asking Jesus to live in your heart, and handing the keys to him. Toss the GPS, pick up the Word of God, and enjoy the ride of a lifetime.

THE TRASH HEAP

Cleanse me with hyssop, and I will be clean; wash
me, and I will be whiter than snow.

Psalm 51:7

Don't you find the little things in life so annoying? I
certainly do. Just this morning I found myself searching
through the kitchen garbage yet again for an inch-long
metal splint the orthopedic doctor had given my son for
a broken finger. Thank God she gave us two of them.
Frustrated by the chaos of our morning routine, I inad-
vertently tossed a splint into the trash for the second time;
only this time, my searching was in vain. I found nothing
but nasty garbage—coffee grounds, used dental floss, dis-
carded orange peels, and guinea pig poop. There was no
rejoicing at my house over the lost splint that was found.

Don't you wonder if sometimes God looks into our
lives and finds himself rummaging through all the garbage, hoping to find his cherished ones who have been

lost? In this world, we are surrounded by so much filth, so many destructive and corrupting influences, that we, too, can get lost in the trash heap. God is never guilty of throwing his beloved ones in the trash. We, ourselves, do that from time to time by dabbling in sin and compromising God's truths.

Sin is not a little thing. No sins are insignificant or benign, even though we may think ours are harmless. The Bible tells us, "All of us have become like one who is unclean, and all our righteous acts are like filthy rags; we all shrivel up like a leaf, and like the wind our sins sweep us away" (Isaiah 64:6). However, just as the orthopedic doctor gave us two splints for my son's broken finger, God gives us second chances day after day. "Because of the LORD's great love we are not consumed, for his compassions never fail. They are new every morning; great is your faithfulness" (Lamentations 3:23–24).

After digging through the garbage to find the splint, I washed my hands thoroughly to clean away all the filth and germs. Only by washing with soap and water were my hands made clean again. The blood of Jesus, shed for us on an old rugged cross, is God's provision for the cleansing of our sins. Nothing but the blood of Jesus can make us whole and restore our righteousness, or right standing, with God.

When God comes looking for you, where will he find you today? Standing knee-deep in a trash heap of sin or clothed with garments of salvation and arrayed in a robe of righteousness (Isaiah 61:10) as his redeemed, beloved child? Step out of the garbage and into his grace. No matter how smelly and dirty you may feel, he is ready to welcome you with open arms and wash you whiter than snow (Psalm 51:7).

ONE THING
IS CERTAIN

I the LORD do not change.

Malachi 3:6

I know a lot of people who are going through changes of one sort or another. I am one of them. Change is something we know well. It happens every day, whether or not we want it to. Change happens to us by force or by choice; we either choose it, or it is thrust upon us with little warning.

What changes are you facing today? A new job, the loss of financial position or health, a new relationship, or the breakup of an existing one? As surely as the seasons change, one thing is certain: God never changes. "He who is the Glory of Israel does not lie or change his mind; for he is not a man, that he should change his mind" (1 Samuel 15:29). That is one truth upon which we can depend.

Dee Dee Wike

Because God never changes, neither does his Word. No matter how tolerant of sin our society becomes, what was sin in the garden of Eden is still sin in our lives today, and we will reap the consequences of our sinful choices.

> Do not be deceived: God cannot be mocked. A man reaps what he sows. The one who sows to please his sinful nature, from that nature will reap destruction; the one who sows to please the Spirit, from the Spirit will reap eternal life.
>
> Galatians 6:7–8

Our sins deserve death, but Christ paid the full price of our redemption long ago when he died in our place on the cross at Calvary. Today, he remains the atoning sacrifice for our sins and the only way to eternal life with our Father in heaven.

Are you looking for a sure thing in your life, something you can hold on to when everything else comes apart at the seams? Look no further than Jesus and the Word of God. Jesus' death on Calvary assures you of an abundant and eternal life with him if you receive him as Savior. The Word of God will guide you into all truth, instruct you in every area of life, and encourage you in your relationship with God and with others. The promises it contains are for you.

Today, take hold of God's grace and the promises of his Word and know, with all certainty, that "if we died with him, we will also live with him; if we endure, we will also reign with him. If we disown him, he will also disown us; if we are faithless, he will remain faithful, for he cannot disown himself" (2 Timothy 2:11–13).

THIRSTY

As the deer pants for streams of water, so my soul
pants for you, O God. My soul thirsts for God, for
the living God. When can I go and meet with God?

Psalm 42:1–2

Although I tried not to let my recent vacation interfere
with my morning practice of sitting before the Lord,
reading his Word, and praying to him, it was difficult to
have a normal quiet time in someone else's home. Once I
returned home, I found myself very thirsty for God and
for his Word and was thankful to be able to meet with
God in the manner I am accustomed—with a steaming
hot cup of coffee, in my favorite chair with my dog by
my side, and before the demands of the day become a
distraction.

I don't think I realized just how much I had missed my
time with the Lord. Although I knew he was with me even

Dee Dee Wike

on vacation, there was something special and refreshing about sitting in his presence in my own little corner and truly focusing on him. I did manage to read a quick devotional the majority of days I was away from home, but my time with the Lord lacked the depth and satisfaction that come with focusing on him for more than five minutes. When I sit down to have my daily quiet time, I am not interested in taking a fast-food approach; I want to eat the whole buffet. Back home again, I was able to finally eat my fill and enjoy the satisfaction of a well-fed soul.

When is the last time you truly hungered for God's presence? Unless you spend time with him daily, you will never know what you have been missing. "Taste and see that the LORD is good; blessed is the man who takes refuge in him" (Psalm 34:8).

IS THERE ANY GOOD NEWS?

> There will be terrible times in the last days. People will be lovers of themselves, lovers of money, boastful, proud, abusive, disobedient to their parents, ungrateful, unholy, without love, unforgiving, slanderous, without self-control, brutal, not lovers of the good, treacherous, rash, conceited, lovers of pleasure rather than lovers of God.
>
> 2 Timothy 3:1–4

Today's headlines say it all: "Shooter Targets Family, Strangers"; "Teen Opens Fire at School in Germany, 10 Dead"; "Madoff Could Face 150-Year Sentence." Our world is spinning out of control, and the news gets worse every day. Murder, greed, the lust for power, abuse—when will it end?

In Matthew 24, Jesus talks about his second coming and all that will take place before he appears to take his chosen ones to heaven. "You will hear of wars and rumors of wars, but see to it that you are not alarmed. Such things must happen, but the end is still to come" (Matthew 24:6). Throughout the entire chapter, Jesus teaches about the signs of the end of the age and what we must do to prepare ourselves for his coming. "Therefore keep watch, because you do not know on what day your Lord will come. So you also must be ready, because the Son of Man will come at an hour when you do not expect him" (vs. 42, 44).

The good news is that Jesus is coming again to take his children home to heaven, where there is no sorrow, pain, murder, greed, war, sexual abuse, disease, or violence. The question is, are *you* ready? Have you asked Jesus to forgive and save you from your sins so that you might be among his chosen ones when he returns to take us home?

No matter what you or I have done, we have this assurance from Jesus himself:

> For God so loved the world that he gave his one and only Son, that whoever believes in him shall not perish but have eternal life. For God did not send his Son into the world to condemn the world, but to save the world through him. Whoever believes in him is not condemned, but whoever does not believe stands condemned already because he has not believed in the name of God's one and only Son.
>
> John 3:16–18

No matter how bad the news is on earth, those of us who have received Christ's salvation can look forward to the day when we will be united with him in heaven, where "there will be no more death or mourning or crying or pain" (Revelation 21:4). We are just passing through...this world is not all there is.

BEING FRUSTRATED CAN BE A GOOD THING

No, in all these things we are more than conquerors through him who loved us. For I am convinced that neither death nor life, neither angels nor demons, neither the present nor the future, nor any powers, neither height nor depth, nor anything else in all creation, will be able to separate us from the love of God that is in Christ Jesus our Lord.

Romans 8:37–39

Recently, after a very long and busy day, I found myself frustrated by all I had failed to accomplish. I decided not to think of that day in negative terms. In fact, for me, the term *frustrated* took on a whole new meaning.

Faith
Remaining
Undeniably
Strong
Through
Reliance
And
Trust
Each
Day

Since life is full of unavoidable challenges, why not develop a new attitude and let frustration strengthen our faith as we rely on and trust God each day? Face it, there isn't much that any of us can do about our circumstances; however, we don't have to let them defeat us. I am tired of negativity, defeat, and failure. I am fighting to win this battle, and I don't intend to lose.

What is it that has you feeling frustrated right now? Pray about it and ask God how to help you turn it around for good. He can use anything, even your most difficult challenge, to strengthen your faith and encourage others.

A PASSIONATE
PURSUIT

Whatever you do, work at it with all your heart, as
working for the Lord, not for men, since you know
that you will receive an inheritance from the Lord
as a reward. It is the Lord Christ you are serving.
                                Colossians 3:23–24

The more I write, the more passionate I become about
writing. That is the way God has wired me, and I am
thankful. For me, writing is more than a gift or a pastime;
it is a platform by which I can communicate God's truths
and encourage his followers.

   One thing I have tried teaching my children is that we
should give our full effort to all that we do, passionately
striving to glorify God. After all, he gave us his best when
he sent Jesus to earth to live as one of us, setting the exam-

ple for how we should live. Jesus held nothing back. He loved the worst of sinners, he healed the undeserving, and he gave everything He had to reach the lost souls of men.

God loved us with so much passion—*lavished* is the term used in 1 John 3:1 to described God's love for us—that he was willing to sacrifice his only Son, Jesus, as the atonement for our sins, making the way for us to spend eternity in his presence. Can you even fathom that kind of love? As much as I love my husband and my own children, I cannot comprehend the kind of love God has for his children.

If God is that passionate about us, should we be any less passionate about sharing the good news with those who are lost? Our lives should be marked by a fervent desire to tell others what God has done for us, how truly faithful and wonderful he is, and how able he is to heal, provide, and guide us through this world of trouble in which we live. His love is unconditional, limitless, and forever.

God is not willing to settle for second place in our hearts. As passionate as I am about my writing, it can never take the place of his presence on the throne of my heart.

What is your passion? Your family, your career, or your relationship with God? Make your passion for God your priority, and you will experience blessing and joy beyond measure.

WHAT IS
YOUR PULPIT?

But you are a chosen people, a royal priesthood, a
holy nation, a people belonging to God, that you
may declare the praises of him who called you out
of darkness into his wonderful light.

1 Peter 2:9

The year 2010 was an incredible and amazing adventure
for me. After years of writing journals and dreaming of
becoming a published author, God opened the door for
the publication of my first book, Good to the Last Drop:
Refreshing Inspiration for Homeschool Moms and Other
Busy Women, and provided me other venues for sharing
his good news of hope and encouragement with others.
The Internet, local and regional newspapers, and my

book have become my pulpit to share the truth with those around me who are hurting or in need of a Savior. I pray that God will eventually provide an open door to speak to individuals and groups about all that he has taught me and is doing in my life and can do in theirs.

However, it isn't necessary to be a writer in order to share the reason for the hope that you have. Each of us has opportunities to bear testimony of God's faithfulness everywhere we go. What is your pulpit? Is it your workplace, your home, or that group of soccer moms you are with every weekend? Is it Facebook or some other social network you frequent on the Internet? Whatever it may be, know that God wants to use you to spread his light and his love in a dark and wounded world.

The Bible tells us that those of us who are followers of Jesus Christ are a royal priesthood, a chosen people, which he has ordained to spread his truth and declare his praises throughout the world. For most of us, technology has decreased the size of our world and put us in touch with people who are spiritually malnourished and need the bread of life, Jesus Christ. What are you doing to feed them? Are you first feeding yourself daily by taking in his Word so that you can, in turn, share it with others? God tells us to be holy in all we do because he is holy (1 Peter 1:15–16). Do your actions and attitude reflect the holiness of God? Actions speak louder than words; let not your actions negate the message of truth God has laid on your heart to share with others.

Take a look around you today. Resolve, in the power of the Holy Spirit, to live as the royal child of God that you are. Open yourself to the possibility that God wants to use you to reach the world with the life-changing message of truth. Find your pulpit and preach God's message by the way you live, love, and serve others.

WHEN OPPORTUNITY KNOCKS

Be very careful, then, how you live—not as unwise but as wise, making the most of every opportunity, because the days are evil. Therefore do not be foolish, but understand what the Lord's will is.

Ephesians 5:15–17

What is it about Mondays? Like the first day of a new year, the start of a new week offers promise and possibility for most. Some dread the return to the work or school week routine; I, on the other hand, view Monday as a chance to make a fresh start, to do better than I did yesterday, and to work toward the goals I have set for myself.

For me, each morning brings with it the hope of starting over and taking advantage of God's golden opportunities.

One of God's greatest gifts to us is time, and I make every effort not to waste it on foolish pursuits and mindless activity. That is not to say that I fill every waking moment with purposeful activity; I have my moments of down time when I choose to watch TV or simply sit and do nothing. But I endeavor to live my life with God's purposes in mind, watching for opportunities to serve and tell others about him. Sometimes that means laying aside the so-called important things I am doing to talk with my teenage son or read a book to my daughter. God uses these divine interruptions to build my relationship with my kids and foster some truly meaningful conversations through which I am able to share spiritual truth and insight with them.

The opportunity to serve God is not *always* super sized; quite often it more resembles a kid's meal with little meat or satisfaction for our adult appetite. But often, God chooses the little things in life to test our commitment and strengthen our relationship with him and others. We often overlook the little opportunities to share God's love by speaking a friendly word to a disgruntled coworker, talking with a lonely friend, or opening the door for a stranger. Everything we do, no matter how important or insignificant it may seem to us, can be a golden opportunity to serve God and minister his grace and mercy to those around us.

As you return to the rat race today, consider the fellow rats around you. Each is on his way to somewhere, shouldering burdens too heavy to bear alone. No matter what day of the week it is, make the most of every opportunity to live for God's purposes, sharing his love and grace with those you may or may not know. Even the little things you do can make a big difference in the lives of those around you.

A MATTER OF THE HEART

Do you not know that your body is a temple of the Holy Spirit, who is in you, whom you have received from God? You are not your own; you were bought at a price. Therefore honor God with your body.

1 Corinthians 6:19–20

Last night after dinner, I took a long overdue walk for the purpose of getting exercise and spending some quality time with my daughter as we enjoyed the beauty of spring and God's creation. As I thanked him for the health and opportunity to get out and walk, I prayed for those who are unable to get out and enjoy such simple pleasures.

My whole life long I have struggled with being over-weight, but over the past several years as I have become more secure in my relationship with the Lord and content with who I am as his child, I have turned less often to food for comfort. That's not to say that I don't occasionally indulge my appetite for chocolate or a signature coffee beverage, but I try to make healthier choices in order to strengthen and sustain my own body for the ministry God has called me to do.

Don't get me wrong—I'm not a health nut. On the contrary, I try to eat a balanced diet, enjoy the foods I crave in moderation, and exercise when my schedule allows. I don't obsess over what I shouldn't eat or how much I should exercise; I simply focus my attention on God instead of food when life gets stressful or my feelings get hurt, and I eat just enough (not too much) when I am physically hungry.

I have learned that health and nutrition truly are matters of the heart, not only because of their potential long-term effects on the physical condition of our hearts, but also because of the underlying spiritual or emotional condition that often dictates what we eat or how we view food. I believe that as we allow God to satisfy our longings and desires, he becomes enough. Food, although necessary to fuel and give health to our bodies, will never satisfy the longings of our hearts. Only God can do that. We are foolish to use food as a substitute for God's love, peace, and comfort.

If you are reading this and you, too, struggle with weight or other substance abuse issues, I encourage you to read Psalm 139 and take note of the way God sees you. You are his cherished creation, his beloved child. He desires to see you not only emotionally and spiritually healthy but physically healthy as well.

I realize that so many of us are busy, sometimes too busy to plan nutritious meals and nurture our bodies. With a little thought, though, we can all make healthier choices. It takes determination and desire to change harmful habits; God can give you that desire and determination if you ask him.

Life is so worth living if you are living it for God. Personally, I don't want to do anything that will subtract one day from the life he has given me to live on this earth. God has a purpose for each of us; if we are not in good health, how can we fulfill that purpose or enjoy the abundant life he desires for each of us?

Today, as you look in the mirror, look at yourself through God's eyes. He loves you and desires to use you for his purposes and glory, no matter what size or shape you are. But he also desires for you to be healthy so you can run the race and win the prize that awaits you.

BRAIN FREEZE

Finally, brothers, whatever is true, whatever is noble, whatever is right, whatever is pure, whatever is lovely, whatever is admirable—if anything is excellent or praiseworthy—think about such things…And the God of peace will be with you.

Philippians 4:8–9

Lately I find myself suffering from brain freeze, not from eating ice cream or drinking something too cold too quickly, but from too much activity and information. Too distracted to even pray effectively, I have asked God to clear the cobwebs and to help me shift my focus from the stuff of everyday life back to my relationship with him.

My mind has been on so many things—a frustrating relationship, publishing deadlines, computer problems at work, and the challenges of parenting a teen and preteen. Like yours, my list is endless. With all that goes on in our lives, how can we reprogram our thinking in order to focus on things of the Lord?

Second Corinthians 10:5 tells us, "We demolish arguments and every pretension that sets itself up against the knowledge of God, and we take captive every thought to make it obedient to Christ." What exactly does that mean? For me, it means analyzing a particular thought or circumstance, applying the truth of Scripture to it, praying about it, and releasing it into God's loving and capable hands. It also means I must continue to love and pray for people despite the changes in their behavior toward me, knowing that I have done all I can to nurture our relationship.

A mind that is hindered from praising God is typically one that is fully of worry, fear, and doubt. Some days I have to really fight the tendency to let fear and worry gain a foothold and steal the joy of my relationship with the Lord.

God knows everything there is to know about our lives. Nothing comes as a surprise to him, so why should we not trust in him to handle the very things that hinder our ability to "approach the throne of grace with confidence, so that we may receive mercy and find grace to help us in our time of need" (Hebrews 4:16)?

SECOND-GUESSING OUR DECISIONS

Fear the LORD, you his saints, for those who fear him lack nothing. The lions may grow weak and hungry, but those who seek the LORD lack no good thing.

Psalm 34:9–10

After my husband gave me the estimate on repairs my car needed—over five hundred dollars—I thought about that nice vacation I just had with my kids in Florida and found myself wishing I hadn't spent the money. Do you ever do that? Do you second-guess decisions you make and wonder if perhaps you should have done things a little differently?

As it was for so many, 2008 was a financially challenging year for our family. We had a lot of unantici-

Dee Dee Wike

pated medical expenses due to our daughter's ankle surgery, expenses that strangled our cash flow and made it necessary to watch and pray over every penny we spent. Christmas was lean, the cupboard was bare, but there was always the knowledge that God was in control. He taught us much about daily trusting in him and never failed to provide what we needed, even when we weren't the wisest of stewards.

Since then, things haven't really changed much. Money is still tight. Cars still break. Life goes on. Do I regret taking that vacation? No, not really, because I know that my children won't be this age forever and that life will continue to throw us curveballs no matter how hard we try to avoid them. Although I certainly could have used my husband's bonus for so many things besides the vacation, my kids and I will always remember the fun we had at Disneyworld and the beach and the long overdue visit with my siblings.

While car repairs are an unavoidable bump in the road to financial freedom, I take great consolation in knowing that God is the same today as he has always been and is faithful to "supply all our needs according to his riches in glory in Christ Jesus" (Philippians 4:19). Even though God is a promise keeper, we are not without responsibility; we must live according to his Word and conduct ourselves in a manner worthy of the gospel of Christ (Philippians 1:27). If we do, we will never have cause to doubt our decisions or regret our choices.

THE SECRET OF A
FAITH THAT WORKS

Now fear the LORD and serve him with all faithfulness. Throw away the gods your forefathers worshiped beyond the River and in Egypt, and serve the LORD. But if serving the LORD seems undesirable to you, then choose for yourselves this day whom you will serve, whether the gods your forefathers served beyond the River, or the gods of the Amorites, in whose land you are living. But as for me and my household, we will serve the LORD.

Joshua 24:14–16

Do you ever wonder why some people appear to have more faith than others or handle the trials of life a little better than perhaps you do? Do you ever wish you could be more like them? What is the secret to having a faith that works rather than a faith that falls short?

Although I have been a Christian for nearly four decades, I haven't always walked in the joy of my salvation. Along the way, I have made more than my share of mistakes and done things that I never thought myself capable of doing. From battling alcoholism to living a lifestyle of unbridled self-indulgence, it is a wonder that somewhere along the way I didn't find myself in jail, or worse, dead. How is it possible for a Christian to live in such a pit of sin, always believing in God but never having the power to overcome or rise above temptation?

Carnal Christianity remains a problem in our churches and is largely the reason why so many people choose to reject Christianity. Why would anyone want to follow in the footsteps of a believer who engages in adulterous relationships, laces their speech with profanity, and treats others with contempt? I was guilty of living as a carnal Christian for many years, rebelling against legalism because I never understood the grace of God and the joy of walking in total surrender to him.

To have a faith that works requires more than just salvation from our sins. Anyone can confess his sins, ask Jesus into his heart, and be saved with the assurance of having eternal life with him in heaven. To live a victorious Christian life, however, requires full surrender of our lives to the Lordship of Christ. If we are to ever have true joy and peace in the midst of our difficult circumstances or understand that God's ways are truly higher than our own, we must lay aside our agenda and submit our plans and our very lives to his will. Only when we put God in the driver's seat and allow him to take us where he wants us to go will we finally begin to enjoy the journey and embrace life as the adventure he intended it to be.

If you have received Jesus as Savior, then praise God, you are headed in the right direction. If you are struggling in your faith and wondering why things don't seem to measure up to your expectations, then ask God to show you what areas of your life you still need to surrender to his Lordship. I promise you that if you will cast down your idols and put him in his rightful place as Lord of your life, you will begin to experience the joy, peace, and purpose that come from aligning yourself with God's will for your life.

Surrender is the key. It is your choice. You can remain a passive observer living a life of mediocrity, or you can choose to grow and live in the abundant life God has waiting for you.

A NEW SONG

He put a new song in my mouth, a hymn of praise to our God. Many will see and fear and put their trust in the Lord.

Psalm 40:3

Lately my daughter has been complaining about songs that keeping going on and on in her mind. She finds this especially troubling at bedtime when she is trying to unwind from the day and go to sleep. How well I can relate to her.

We all have things that we tend to mull over in our minds, whether or not we want to. Whether it is a problem that continues to plague us or an old hurt that we cannot seem to get over, we tend to hang on to things that only serve to agitate us and steal our joy.

A few weeks ago, my children and I were participants in a neighbor's science project. The goal of her project was to demonstrate how different types of music affect our blood pressure. Think about it—when you are feeling down, don't you sometimes play upbeat music in an effort to lift your spirit? I know I do.

It is so hard to be consistently positive and joyful in this day and age with all the challenges we must face, yet most of us know at least one person who seems able to rise above his problems and maintain a positive outlook. What is his secret? How can he whistle a happy tune when the rest of us are singing the blues?

Our answer lies in the Word of God. The Bible tells us, "Let the word of Christ dwell in you richly as you teach and admonish one another with all wisdom, and as you sing psalms, hymns and spiritual songs with gratitude in your hearts to God" (Colossians 3:16). As far as I am concerned, the surest antidote for a rotten mindset is to thank God for the good things in my life rather than focus on the bad. As I choose to think about things that are noble, right, pure, lovely, admirable, excellent, or praiseworthy, I find that God restores my joy (Philippians 4:8). If we are to be transformed in the renewing of our minds (Romans 12:2), we must take the time to read and know God's Word so we can confidently stand on his promises and experience his provision, healing, and peace.

What music will you choose to listen to today? Rather than listen to the sound of your own voice replay your woes like a broken record, tune into the sweet voice of Jesus and the love song he has written for you in his Word.

Lord, satisfy us in the morning with your unfailing love, that we may sing for joy and be glad all our days (Psalm 90:14).

SOMEONE I DON'T WANT TO BE

So I find this law at work: when I want to do good,
evil is right there with me. For in my inner being I
delight in God's law; but I see another law at work
in the members of my body, waging war against
the law of my mind and making me a prisoner of
the law of sin at work within my members. What
a wretched man am I!

Romans 7:21–24

Do you ever have those days when you are simply fed up
and angry? Days when you are prone to fuss about every
little thing for no apparent reason? When I can't shake
the bad mood and focus on more positive things, I begin
to dislike the person in the mirror and wish I could be
someone else.

The apostle Paul was a conflicted individual, just as we sometimes are. He had his moments of struggle over sin and self-loathing, yet God still loved him. Despite his frustration, he could say with certainty, "There is now no condemnation for those who are in Christ Jesus, because through Christ Jesus the law of the Spirit of life set me free from the law of sin and death" (Romans 8:1–2).

Much of the anger we feel at times is the result of a heart that is broken over people and things we cannot fix. But then, when did fixing anyone become our responsibility? Still we are not very patient when it comes to God's slow timing in changing those people for whom we have prayed. Perhaps we are the ones God needs to make over.

> Create in me a pure heart, O God, and renew a steadfast spirit within me. Do not cast me from your presence or take your Holy Spirit from me. Restore to me the joy of your salvation and grant me a willing spirit, to sustain me. A broken and contrite heart, O God, you will not despise.
>
> Psalm 51:10–12, 17

TAKING MATTERS INTO OUR OWN HANDS

They fell down with their faces to the ground, and the glory of the LORD appeared to them. "You and your brother Aaron are to speak to the rock while they watch, and it will yield its water. You will bring water for them from the rock and provide drink for the community and their livestock." Moses and Aaron summoned the assembly in front of the rock...Then Moses raised his hand and struck the rock twice with his staff. But the LORD said to Moses and Aaron, "Because you did not trust Me to show My holiness in the sight of the Israelites, you will not bring this assembly into the land I have given them."

Numbers 20:6, 8, 10–12, HCSB

Sometimes when I read God's Word, a passage will stop me in my tracks. The story of Moses striking the rock in the twentieth chapter of Numbers recently caught my attention. Although the excerpt above gives you the gist of what transpired, I encourage you to pick up your Bible and read the passage in its entirety. The following thoughts came to mind as I read this passage:

1. "They fell down with their faces to the ground, and the glory of the LORD appeared to them" (v. 6). When confronted with the problem of an angry, thirsty community, Moses and Aaron sought the LORD humbly, bowing before him. As they humbled themselves to pray and seek God's solution, he revealed his glory to them. How long did they have to wait in God's presence in order to see his glory revealed? I am convinced that sometimes we fail to see God's glory or experience his mighty power because we don't wait long enough.

2. "You and your brother Aaron are to speak to the rock while they watch, and it will yield its water" (v. 8). "Then Moses raised his hand and struck the rock twice with his staff" (v. 11). God said one thing; Moses did entirely another. Are we not the same? When God tells us to do something, we often question whether his

ways are actually higher than ours (Isaiah 55:9). When we decide that perhaps our way of doing something would be more effective, we take matters into our own hands. We fail to trust that God will do what he has said, so we take it upon ourselves to solve the problem rather than trust and obey his commands.

3. "But the LORD said to Moses and Aaron, 'Because you did not trust Me to show My holiness in the sight of the Israelites, you will not bring this assembly into the land I have given them'" (v. 12). It never fails. When we disobey God, we suffer the consequences. Moses and Aaron attempted to solve the problem as they saw fit. Because of their disobedience, they were not allowed to enter the Promised Land. The promise of a better life was shattered by a simple act of disobedience.

As I look at this passage, I can see examples in my own life of times I have taken matters in my own hands and attempted to fix what only God can. We are such an impatient people, and our impatience often gets us into trouble. Our mounting consumer debt is proof of that. I suppose it is true that "good things come to those who wait."

What is it that you are seeking from the Lord today? A better job? The salvation of a loved one? The healing of a heart broken by someone you love? Rather than strive to solve the problem on your own, "Stand firm and see the deliverance the LORD will give you...do not be afraid; do not be discouraged" (2 Chronicles 20:17). "Humble yourselves, therefore, under God's mighty hand, that he may lift you up in due time. Cast all your anxiety on him because he cares for you" (1 Peter 5:6-7).

NEARLY LOST

Trust in the LORD with all your heart and lean not on your own understanding; in all your ways acknowledge him, and he will make your paths straight.

Proverbs 3:5–6

When my brother suggested I use his GPS to navigate the streets of Orlando rather than rely on maps and hand-written directions, I politely refused, thinking I was well-equipped to reach my destination using the maps I had printed off the Internet. I soon learned the hard way that the distraction of reading a map at night in a strange city is a recipe for disaster.

While attempting to follow a set of printed directions to my brother's house I prepared to make a left turn, look-ing in my rear and side-view mirrors before entering the turn lane. My confidence that I was finally headed in the right direction was shattered by the scraping of metal as a car I hadn't seen collided with me in the turn lane.

Lost took on a different meaning as I prayed my way through what could have been a very bad situation. The man who hit our car had just come off a twelve-hour shift, was from out of town, swore with every breath he took, and seemed totally intent on not calling the police or swapping insurance. He cursed; I prayed. Although I knew better, I followed him from the intersection into a nearby parking lot because he insisted that, for safety's sake, we should move the cars. As he opened his trunk, I prayed it was not to pull out a gun to shoot me in front of my children. He was that mad. When I saw that it was a crowbar he was after, I prayed that he would not turn from the task of popping out the dents in his car to pummeling me with it. I sensed he was lost; I was afraid my life would be taken from me while my children watched on a dark Orlando street.

I never ceased to pray. I held on to the promises of Scripture that God would protect me. He did. As I prayed and let God work, the irate driver of the other vehicle softened in his demeanor, and we parted ways, oddly with an embrace and his apology. The whole situation was quite bizarre.

Had I leaned on my own understanding and behaved as a distraught victim, I am convinced that the ending would have turned out differently, and badly, for my children and me. As it was, I leaned on my understanding of God, watched his power transform a potentially violent and angry man into one concerned about the welfare of

Dee Dee Wike

my children, and drove away with hardly any damage to my car.

God doesn't want us to wander through life without direction or a sense of security. Everything we need has been provided for us in his Word. If you are afraid, lost, or simply in need of encouragement, pick up your Bible, read it, and believe that it was written for your good and your protection. God's Word is never wrong, and his directions will never leave you lost.

THE PROMISE KEEPER

God is not a man, that he should lie, nor a son of man, that he should change his mind. Does he speak and then not act? Does he promise and not fulfill?

Numbers 23:18–19

Often I have written of God's faithfulness to keep his Word. I know I must sound like a broken record, but I have seen evidence of his faithfulness time and time again, not only in my life, but in the lives of others who know and serve him. As I have memorized and learned to pray Scripture, God has worked powerfully in my life to guide, protect, provide, and impart grace and wisdom when needed. His Word has given me peace in times of peril (see "Nearly Lost"), the assurance of provision in times of

Dee Dee Wike

need, and words of comfort and encouragement for those who are struggling with their own challenges.

We live in such a chaotic and troubled world. With all that is taking place around us—financial woes, unemployment, job stress, broken relationships, disease, and even death—what else but God can we hold on to? When we know God's Word, we know *him* and learn that we can trust him.

I know there are those who doubt God because of circumstances and issues, which somehow seem hopeless. At times, even I am prone to doubt because of my own humanity. But his Word is truth, and God will never go back on his Word. When we pray God's Word back to him, how can he not hear and answer our prayers? Sometimes we don't get an immediate answer, but even God's Word addresses that: "The Lord is not slow in keeping his promise, as some understand slowness. He is patient with you, not wanting anyone to perish, but everyone to come to repentance" (2 Peter 3:9).

Much of our doubt in God's commitment to his promises is a result of our tendency to take his Word out of context and somehow make it fit our lives. Hebrews 4:12 tells us, "The word of God is living and active. Sharper than any double-edged sword, it penetrates even to dividing soul and spirit, joints and marrow; it judges the thoughts and attitudes of the heart." There is an inherent danger in misusing God's Word by failing to carefully study and correctly handle the word of truth (2 Timothy 2:15).

It has been said that the Bible is God's handbook for living, but to me, it is so much more than that. It is the key to unlocking the very heart and character of God, the one who lavished his love on us (1 John 3:1) and gave us his only Son to be our Savior (John 3:16). Do you know him? Have you read his Word lately? It is God's love letter to you and a hope chest full of promise and possibilities.

FAULTY PROGRAMMING

.

The mind of sinful man is death, but the mind controlled by the Spirit is life and peace.

Romans 8:6

What do you do when your mind thinks about things it shouldn't? It is a problem we all face at one time or another. Our brains are like a computer operating on the "Garbage In, Garbage Out" principle. So much of the negative and sinful thinking we are guilty of results from our willful disobedience to God and our practice of reading, looking at, and listening to things we shouldn't.

While I try carefully to refrain from negatively programming my thoughts with bad input, I still find that often I need to debug my memories of the past, whether good or bad. Like a computer virus, I find that my thought life contains some stealth programs that occasionally infiltrate my emotions, causing me to eventually crash. Satan knows how powerful a weapon the mind can be and how easily it can be used against us to hinder our walk with God. He will stop at nothing to clutter up our minds with garbage so that we are rendered ineffective as Christians.

What is the solution? What can we do to rewrite the programs driving our thought process? First of all, when we recognize our faulty thinking, we need to immediately confess it. Quite often, my worst thoughts play themselves out in my dreams. Some mornings, I find myself having to confess sinful thoughts before my feet even hit the floor.

Second, we need to cast down our sinful thoughts by meditating on Scripture and praying it back to the Lord. To do that requires knowledge of God's Word gained by spending time reading and memorizing it. The Bible tells us:

> Do not conform any longer to the pattern of this world, but be transformed by the renewing of your mind. Then you will be able to test and approve what God's will is—his good, pleasing and perfect will.
>
> Romans 12:2

We cannot know the will of God if we don't know the Word of God.

Third, we need to pray about, and in some cases, avoid the circumstances or people that trigger our negative thinking. When that is not possible, we need to pray for God's

Dee Dee Wike

protection against thoughts and actions that could compromise our walk with him and our witness to other people.

> Search me, O God, and know my heart; test me and know my anxious thoughts. See if there is any offensive way in me, and lead me in the way everlasting.
>
> Psalm 139:23–24

EVERYWHERE I GO

Where can I go from your Spirit? Where can I flee from your presence? If I go up to the heavens, you are there; if I make my bed in the depths, you are there.

Psalm 139:7–8

As my kids have gotten older, I have become more familiar with the emergency room at a local hospital. Between broken arms and lacerations, I have made at least one or two annual trips to the ER. Recently, I had to meet my husband there as he was checked for symptoms of a heart attack. Then, not many days after that, it was my turn. As was the case with him, my pain, though symptomatic of a cardiac issue, turned out to be something totally unrelated—a sprained shoulder. A few days on steroids and pain medication were prescribed to have me feeling good as new.

Dee Dee Wike

The emergency room was so packed that I never did make it into a room. Even in the midst of the chaos, I had a keen awareness of God's presence and peace. Never was I fearful. In fact, I was so at peace that I eventually sent my family home to get some rest, having the assurance that God would be with me. While there, I had an opportunity to observe and pray for the many patients who came in for treatment, the medical staff who sprang into action when one of the patients went into full cardiac arrest, and all the family members who were there to see about their loved ones.

My visit to the ER was an inconvenience and expense to me, one that probably could have been avoided had I simply taken a couple of ibuprofen and waited until morning. Yet I believe that my trip there was one of God's divine appointments to teach me how faithful he is, how blessed I am, and how important it is to pray for those in need. It was an opportunity to surrender to his will, even though it meant giving up my Saturday night, losing a lot of sleep, and being surrounded by some very sick people.

As you go through your day, pray that God will give you a heightened sense of his presence and a greater sensitivity to the needs of those around you. Know that if God puts you in a difficult or unpleasant situation, it is because he has something to teach you or something that he needs for you to do for him or for someone else. Nothing in life is random; there is a reason for everything we experience. Rest in the promise that wherever God sends you, he has a purpose and will be with you every step of the way.

TOO MUCH OR TOO LITTLE?

Give me neither poverty nor riches, but give me only my daily bread. Otherwise, I may have too much and disown you and say, "Who is the LORD?" Or I may become poor and steal, and so dishonor the name of my God.

Proverbs 30:8–9

As many families do, we live paycheck-to-paycheck and are always glad to see the funds reflected in our bank balance when payday finally arrives. Unfortunately, the business of daily living is expensive, and the thrill of the paycheck, short-lived. In less than twenty-four hours, I managed to spend every penny of my husband's check on just the necessities of life, and we still came up short.

We all know of entertainment and sports celebrities who make millions of dollars for what they do and perhaps never worry about their day-to-day expenses. I don't envy the wealth of professional athletes or movie stars, but I would sure like enough money to comfortably make it from payday to payday without having to think about how I am going to pay for my son's driver education course or his summer youth group trip or whether or not I can afford to have my dog groomed and still buy groceries to feed my family for the next two weeks.

When the relief of a paycheck gives way to discouragement over how quickly the money goes, I can confidently rely on Scripture and God's promises that he will indeed take care of our daily needs. God's Word provides clear instruction on money, stewardship, and work and is filled with his promises to take care of those who follow him.

No matter how hard I try to prudently manage the resources God entrusts to us, there never seems to be enough to go around. As I cry out to the one who is sufficient to supply all our daily needs, I know that he will provide what we need as we give him first place in our lives (Matthew 6:33–34).

BE PREPARED

Preach the Word: be prepared in season and out of season; correct, rebuke and encourage—with great patience and careful instruction.

2 Timothy 4:2

One night, I had a very vivid nightmare. After having been invited to address a group of women regarding my new book and my faith, I walked up to the podium with nothing in my hands—no notes, no Bible, no message. I was mortified.

With my first book scheduled for publication later that year, I had been praying about how God might use the book and my writing ministry. Many times I had envisioned myself as the keynote speaker at a women's event somewhere, encouraging ladies to read and study the Word and apply it to their daily lives. That would require a great deal of preparation on my part.

Life is full of situations and circumstances that can easily derail us in our faith walk if we are not firmly grounded in the Word of God. Worries over money and children, bad news regarding a loved one's or our own health, or just the stresses of everyday living can take their toll on our spirits if we are not aligned with God's purposes and taking in daily doses of Scripture. If we are to walk as victorious Christians in these troubling times, we must increase our knowledge of and be obedient to the Word of God.

Not only do we need to know the Word of God in order to face our own challenges, we also need to be able to use the Scriptures to edify and encourage others. When someone asks how it is that we are able to get through a particular difficulty, we need to be able to give them a reason for the hope that we have (1 Peter 3:15).

Are you prepared to joyfully and victoriously face your challenges today? If not, take a few minutes to arm yourself with the Word of God and prayer. Then,

> Do everything without complaining or arguing, so that you may become blameless and pure, children of God without fault in a crooked and depraved generation, in which you shine like stars in the universe as you hold out the word of life.
>
> Philippians 2:14–16

SLOW DOWN!
REDUCED
SPEED AHEAD

You were wearied by all your ways, but you would not say, "It is hopeless." You found renewal of your strength, and so you did not faint.

Isaiah 57:10

Is it just me, or does the pace of life get more hectic with the passing of time? Sometimes when I have an especially busy week, I feel like a sprinkler in the heat of August, working furiously to water the grass, only to see it evaporate before it hits the ground. What God can accomplish with a simple rain, it takes hours for my sprinkler to do.

Dee Dee Wike

Isn't all our effort like that? We run constantly, endeavoring to cover all the bases but somehow fall short and wear ourselves out in the process. We haven't yet learned to stop and smell the roses.

Truly I have been wearied by all my ways this week. I have been so busy that I have neglected important matters, made silly mistakes, and failed to enjoy God's simple blessings. My spark plugs are misfiring; it's time for a tune-up.

The beauty of having a quiet time each morning is that it gives us a chance to be tuned up and refreshed so we can face the demands of each new day. By slowing down enough to bask in God's presence and the promises of his Word, we find the rest and hope our souls need to take on life's challenges. At the end of an especially busy day, taking just a few minutes to sit in God's presence, reflect on our day, and read a passage or two of Scripture can quiet our minds better than any sleep aid on the market.

Rather than try to navigate life's busy highway today, give God the keys, leave the driving to him, and simply enjoy the ride.

WE ALL HAVE OUR MOMENTS

Fathers, do not exasperate your children; instead,
bring them up in the training and instruction of
the Lord.

Ephesians 6:4

Is there anything more stressful for a parent than conflict
with their children? Some days it seems our children are
bent on doing the exact opposite of everything we ask of
them. As patience wears thin we find ourselves exasper-
ated and argumentative rather than calm and graceful in
the way we communicate with our children, no matter
what age they are.

As parents, we would do well to remember that "a
gentle answer turns away wrath, but a harsh word stirs
up anger" (Proverbs 15:1). The next time you find yourself
in the heat of the battle with your kids, try using a quiet

Dee Dee Wike

voice when defending your position. Arguing never solves anything and some battles simply are not worth fighting. If you simply cannot remain calm, turn around and walk out of the room until the tension dissipates. It takes two to tango. An argument will die down if you remove the anger which fuels it.

Being a parent is difficult at times. To firmly stand our ground when we would rather give in just to maintain a little peace is something we all struggle with on occasion. Sometimes we make mistakes in the way we handle an argument. When that happens it is important that we not only acknowledge our fault and ask God's forgiveness, but also that we humble ourselves, apologize to our children, and ask theirs. When we do, our children recognize that we, too, sometimes struggle and make mistakes and that we need their forgiveness as much as they need ours.

God is our heavenly Father, and our children are his children. Just as God want his best for us, we want so much for our children to grow up loving and obeying God, not making mistakes that will cause them and us pain. Despite our best efforts to train them up in the way they should go, our children may very well deviate from God's purposes and plans for their lives and learn things the hard way, just like we did. Our prayer must be that if they do step outside God's perfect will, they will quickly find their way home to the arms of their heavenly Father.

For as long as they are with us, let us strive to love our children the way God loves them and cherish the moments we have now, knowing that before long they will leave our nests and make homes of their own.

LESSONS FROM MY GARDEN

I am the true vine and my Father is the gardener. He cuts off every branch in me that bears no fruit, while every branch that does bear fruit he trims clean so that it will be even more fruitful. You are already clean because of the word I have spoken to you. Remain in me and I will remain in you. This is to my Father's glory, that you bear much fruit, showing yourselves to be my disciples.

John 15:1–4, 8

Many of the women I know are in the midst of spring-cleaning their homes; I am not one of them. My idea of spring-cleaning is to spend hours and hours on my knees pulling the weeds out of my flowerbeds so that my lovely azaleas are not eclipsed by unsightly weeds. I let my husband do the spring-cleaning inside.

Dee Dee Wike

Yesterday, I spent about seven hours weeding a portion of my flowerbeds as I enjoyed the beautiful spring weather and God's sweet presence. Normally, I don't dread the prospect of weeding my beds because I have a great garden tool that makes the job relatively easy. This year, however, I noticed that many of my weeds were of a more stubborn variety than I have previously encountered. As I tediously worked to remove them, I began to get a vivid picture of sin and just how pervasive it can be.

While some of the weeds in my garden came up rather easily, many had taken root with a vengeance, requiring that I scoop out a layer of topsoil in order to get rid of the weeds, roots and all. It dawned on me that sin is quite like that—some sins are relatively easy to deal with and eradicate, while others require years of effort to uproot them from our lives. The more embedded the weeds are, the greater the amount of dirt that is attached to their roots. The same can be said of our sin—the greater the sin, the greater the guilt and shame we may suffer. The good news, though, is that Jesus has already paid the price for all our sins, great or small, and that "if we confess our sins, he is faithful and just and will forgive us our sins and purify us from all unrighteousness" (1 John 1:9).

Weeding is not my only annual spring garden ritual. I also prune my rose bushes every March so that my roses are more beautiful and prolific. Until a year ago, we had an apple tree in the backyard. I am sure the previous owners must have enjoyed its fruit for a while, but years of not pruning the tree resulted in a diminishing crop of apples.

Because the tree had become unsightly and unfruitful, we decided to remove it to make way for a vegetable garden.

What will be growing in your garden this year? Beautiful flowers or pesky weeds? While you're on your hands and knees pulling those weeds out, ask the Lord to show you what areas of your life need a little pruning. Ask him to make you a fruitful vine, bearing fruit that will last (John 15:16).

Dee Dee Wike

PUTTING FORTH
THE EFFORT

Let us therefore make every effort to do what leads to peace and to mutual edification.

Romans 14:19

Life can be very labor intensive. Even relatively simple tasks like taking out the trash can require much effort if, for instance, the bag breaks and leaves a mess to clean up. Distractions break our concentration and before long we find ourselves expending more effort trying to pick up where we left off than we would have needed to complete the job on the first attempt.

When I looked up the word *effort* in my Bible's concordance, I didn't really expect to find it there. Nevertheless, there were several scriptures incorporating that word. In nearly every instance, effort expended was associated with a positive result. When we put in the effort to accomplish things well, quite often we experience less stress and frustration and a greater sense of accomplishment.

Maintaining good relationships requires perhaps more effort than anything else in life. It takes effort and a great deal of time to nurture our relationships with others and with God. If you are willing to put forth the effort, though, especially in building your relationship with the Lord, you will reap the riches of God's peace, protection, and provision. Putting forth the effort to be rightly related with God will help everything else in life fall into place.

Dee Dee Wike

FROM THE MUNDANE TO THE INSANE

But be very careful to keep the commandment and the law that Moses the servant of the LORD gave you: to love the LORD your God, to walk in all his ways, to obey his commands, to hold fast to him and to serve him with all your heart and all your soul.

Joshua 22:5

As I was making and praying through my to-do list for the week, I noticed that some of the items I jotted down were mundane in nature and that the number of things I needed to accomplish was absolutely insane. Yet that is typical for most of us. We all have tasks we don't particularly enjoy doing and more things to do than time will allow. When we focus on all we have to do, we can easily become overwhelmed and disheartened. The key in avoiding those negative, energy-depleting feelings is to focus not on what we have to do but on the ones we are serving and on the God whose glory we are ultimately striving for in the first place.

God created time and equipped us each with special gifts to be used for his glory and for the benefit of those around us. He provides us everything we need to do the work he has called us to do. He expects us to work hard, rest from our labors, and serve others sacrificially, not simply when it is convenient. He gave us Jesus, God in human flesh, as a model of servanthood and the Holy Spirit to supply us with the power, wisdom, love, and grace we need each day to fulfill God's plan and purpose for our lives.

As you make your own to-do list today or this week, ask God for wisdom to know not only what you need to do but also how to balance everything you need to accomplish. Ask him for the grace and patience to work diligently, not so you can check everything off your list, but rather to show the world what a great God you serve. Let your achievements be for his glory, not your own.

Above all, from the mundane tasks to the insane amount of work you face this week, surrender each and every task to God. Know that he is in control. Trust him to accomplish through you the things that truly matter. At all times, stay focused on him, thanking him for the strength to do what he has called you to do and giving him the glory for all he allows you to accomplish.

As you go about your work, remain sensitive to the leading of the Holy Spirit and to the needs of those around you. It is easy to become so wrapped up in all we have to do that we forget there are people around us who need to see the light and love of Christ reflected in our lives. Serve willingly, not because you have to but to honor the one who first loved and served us.

THREE STEPS FORWARD, TWO STEPS BACK

Not only so, but we also rejoice in our sufferings, because we know that suffering produces perseverance; perseverance, character; and character, hope. And hope does not disappoint us, because God has poured out his love into our hearts by the Holy Spirit, whom he has given us.

Romans 5:3–5

Sometimes life is not a very comfortable place for me. Quite frankly, I grow tired of the same old three steps forward, two steps back dance that hinders my progress some days. Do you ever feel like that?

Dee Dee Wike

The only way I can cope with the constant stress of living in twenty-first century America is to hold on to the only truth I know—God's Word. When my children do things that are harmful to themselves and hurtful to me, I choose to stand firm as a parent when I would rather give up, knowing that I am engaged in a battle of eternal significance. God is building their character and mine. Although it is sometimes a painful process for all of us, I am committed to fight against the enemy who seeks to steal, kill, and destroy the good that is in them and the joy that is in me. It's a very hard battle some days, one I can only fight by keeping my eyes focused on the one who is working all things together for their good and mine.

Money is lousy dance partner. Living paycheck to paycheck is not the same as dancing cheek to cheek with a partner you love. Money comes and quickly goes, never staying long enough to do any real good. Just when we think we're making some headway in paying off debt, a medical situation or unexpected repair of some sort cuts in on the dance and leaves us reeling. Thank God Jehovah Jireh is ready to step in and shelter us in the arms of his loving embrace.

As you waltz through life, who will be holding you? In Jeremiah 31:4, the Lord said to the Israelites, "I will build you up again and you will be rebuilt, O Virgin Israel. Again you will take up your tambourines and go out to dance with the joyful." Let the Lord of the dance hold you, build you up, and restore your joy today.

PEACE LIKE A RIVER

For this is what the LORD says: "I will extend peace to her like a river, and the wealth of nations like a flooding stream; you will nurse and be carried on her arm and dandled on her knees. As a mother comforts her child, so will I comfort you."

Isaiah 66:12–13

On a picture-perfect spring day despite a crystal clear sky and a gentle, cool breeze, I felt shrouded by a cloud of despair. Dreading another day of parenting challenges and my children's waning interest in school, my only thought was, We need a field trip to the river! Driving downtown and sitting on the banks of the Mississippi River would not solve my dilemma, but it might at least make me feel better.

As I sat with my children watching barges and drift-wood float downstream, I envisioned my problems float-ing away as well. I wish it were that simple! Lying on the blanket with my eyes closed and my face turned toward the sun, I rested and prayed for answers, peace, wisdom, and grace to make it through the rest of my day.

In running to the river that day, I was in fact running to God, my only source of peace in times of trouble. There are many verses of Scripture, which associate water with peace and calm. One such passage is Psalm 23:2–3: "He makes me lie down in green pastures, he leads me beside quiet waters, he restores my soul."

Is it any wonder that many of us flock to beaches and lakes to find a little tranquility? The solution to our problems will never be found in an ocean, lake, or river. Only Jesus, the living water, can give us peace when the demands and stress of daily life become overwhelming. Knowing God's Word gives us a foothold when the river rages around us. As we delight in his Word and meditate on it day and night, we will be like trees planted by streams of water, yielding our fruit in due season (Psalm 1:2–3). Our problems will not magically be washed away, but God promises that in him, we will find peace.

DO YOU HAVE A UPS?

Now to him who is able to do immeasurably more than all we ask or imagine, according to his power that is at work within us, to him be glory in the church and in Christ Jesus throughout all generations, forever and ever! Amen.

Ephesians 3:20–21

For many people who own computers, particularly those who use them for business, having a UPS, or uninterruptible power supply, is very important. Having a UPS ensures that when the power goes out unexpectedly, there is enough backup power to save your data and files before the computer actually shuts down. It is insurance against the loss of critical files. If you have ever suffered the loss of

Dee Dee Wike

important files, you know it is something you don't want to have happen twice.

Those of us living in the trenches of everyday life have available to us a divine UPS through our relationship with Jesus, whose power at work in us never fails no matter how stormy life gets. Through the person of the Holy Spirit, who indwells us at the moment of our salvation, we have the power and wisdom and every other resource we need to walk in victory and joy, no matter how difficult our circumstances may be. The promises of God's Word, the guidance of the Holy Spirit, and the love of Christ for those around us are powerful forces that can have a significant, eternal impact on the lives of those we encounter every day.

When Christ died on Calvary's cross to save us from our sins, many of those who witnessed his death lost hope that salvation and redemption would ever come to mankind. They didn't understand the prophecies that were to be fulfilled on the day of his resurrection or the kind of power they could possess as his followers. The Bible speaks clearly of the "power that is at work in us" (Ephesians 3:20), the power by which "God raised the Lord from the dead" (1 Corinthians 6:14). Paul, writing to the Philippians, said, "I want to know Christ and the power of his resurrection and the fellowship of sharing in his sufferings, becoming like him in his death, and so, somehow, to attain to the resurrection of the dead" (Philippians 3:10–11). For Paul, knowing Christ and experiencing the power of his resurrection became of paramount importance to him. So it should be for us who call ourselves Christians.

So often we fail to realize just how much power is available to us. Some days it seems life comes at us from a thousand different directions, and we struggle just to put one foot in front of the other. That shouldn't be the case with us. When Christ died, he left us with a counselor, a comforter, and a UPS we know as the Holy Spirit. When he arose from the dead, he conquered death and became alive forever. He lives within each of us who has received him as Savior. Nothing can separate us from his love or diminish his power in us.

The world needs to know our Savior. The best way for them to know Jesus is to see his power at work in us. Are you plugged into your UPS? Is your light shining brightly so the world can see your good works and glorify your Father who is in heaven? (Matthew 5:16). If not, pray:

> That you may live a life worthy of the Lord and may please him in every way: bearing fruit in every good work, growing in the knowledge of God, being strengthened with all power according to his glorious might so that you may have great endurance and patience, and joyfully giving thanks to the Father, who has qualified you to share in the inheritance of the saints in the kingdom of light.
>
> Colossians 1:10–12

Dee Dee Wike

STUBBY THE SQUIRREL

I praise you because I am fearfully and wonderfully made; your works are wonderful, I know that full well.

Psalm 139:14

It was a beautiful spring day as I took my morning walk. Traveling my usual route, I noticed a most peculiar sight as I walked along a neighbor's fence. Perched atop the planks was a squirrel, which was missing nearly his entire tail. It wasn't merely thin from having been plucked to make a nest. Rather, it was nothing more than a two-inch long stub. Poor squirrel! I shudder to think how he must have lost his tail and wonder if he felt inferior to the other squirrels in the neighborhood. After all, a squirrel's plumy tail is his most distinctive feature.

Somehow I don't believe that animals go around comparing themselves to one another the way humans do. That is a blessing for them. Yet we humans can't seem to help comparing ourselves to one another and developing feelings of inferiority. Ever since the serpent made Adam and Eve feel inferior to God and tempted them to eat of the tree of the knowledge of good and evil, we have been selling ourselves short and looking for ways to make ourselves feel better about ourselves. We are guilty of deriving our significance from the standards set by society, Hollywood, and false religions rather from what God's Word says about us.

One of my favorite psalms is Psalm 139. The entire psalm speaks of how incredibly special we are to our maker and how intimately he is acquainted with all our ways. He made us the way we are for a reason, ordaining each of our days before one of them came to be (v. 16). His thoughts concerning us are precious (v. 17), and he lives to intercede for us at his Father's right hand. I love the way Beth Moore expresses that thought: Jesus is sitting at God's right hand talking to his Father about us.

God doesn't qualify our beauty according to our body shape, complexion, or hair color. He qualifies our beauty according to the condition of our hearts and spirit.

> Your beauty should not come from outward adornment, such as braided hair and the wearing of gold jewelry and fine clothes. Instead, it should be that of your inner self, the unfading beauty of a gentle and quiet spirit, which is of great worth in God's sight.

Dee Dee Wike

Truly, "pretty is as pretty does."

God created each of us as unique human beings—one of a kind, never to be duplicated in all of eternity. The next time you are tempted to compare yourself with someone else, keep that in mind: there's no one else quite like you.

A MOST UNUSUAL EASTER

> Then their eyes were opened and they recognized him, and he disappeared from their sight. They asked each other, "Were not our hearts burning within us while he talked with us on the road and opened the Scriptures to us?"
>
> Luke 24:31–32

On Good Friday morning, my daughter and I drove to Arkansas to spend Easter weekend with my mom and prepare her tax return before the April 15 deadline.

Mom recently retired to her mountain retreat, although she continues to work full-time at Wal-Mart. Although she was scheduled to have Easter Sunday off, because she worked until midnight on Saturday, I felt she needed rest more than I needed to go to church, so for the first time in my life I chose not to attend church on Easter Sunday. Besides, the weather was forecast to be stormy. So we stayed home in the cozy comfort of her little house in the woods, where we watched a classic Adrian Rogers Easter sermon on television. I learned that while nothing replaces being at church on Easter morning, it is indeed possible to worship God while watching a TV sermon in pajamas.

When the first chord of music played, I was moved to tears by a familiar song that had become a favorite of mine. The selection brought back sweet memories of our church's Easter production many years ago. How we worshipped our Savior during our Easter pageant.

Did I miss being at church on Easter Sunday? Sure, but I enjoyed my time with Mom so much. She will not always be with me, but the Lord has promised that he will be with me forever. Because he has risen and given me the gift of his Holy Spirit, my worship of him is no longer confined to the sanctuary of my home church.

Jesus still appears to his followers today. Whether we worship him in a cathedral or in a little cabin in the woods, our hearts are stirred as he reveals himself to us through the pages of Scripture. May your heart burn within you today as you read God's Word and worship him wherever you are.

LET IT BEGIN WITH ME

Fix these words of mine in your hearts and minds; tie them as symbols on your hands and bind them on your foreheads. Teach them to your children, talking about them when you sit at home and when you walk along the road, when you lie down and when you get up.

Deuteronomy 11:18–19

As a worship leader for our youth group in the seventies, I remember singing the song, "Let There Be Peace on Earth." The last line of the song read, "Let it begin with me." Now that I am the mother of a teenager and a preteen, I realize that the society in which they are growing up is a far less peaceful place than the one I knew at their age. My fervent prayer is that despite all the worldly influences around them, they will grow to follow the Lord and become peacemakers in their generation.

On Election Day, I wrote an article entitled "God Bless America," a message God laid on my heart as we faced a historic presidential election. I believed then, as I do now, that if there is to be any positive change in the direction of our society, it will come only as Christians begin to pray for our country, live according to God's biblical standards, and influence others to do the same. Those others include our children.

Parenting our children in modern-day America is perhaps the most difficult challenge some of us will ever face. As much as we want our kids to get along with us, we must remember that we are their parents, not their friends. Even as they grow toward adulthood and the independence that goes along with maturity, we must continue to teach, pray for, and guide them, holding them accountable to God's laws and standards for living. Parenting is an endless job, even though our role changes as our kids transition from childhood into adulthood.

If we can help our children understand that we don't make the rules—God does—then parenting them with the goal of helping them become peace-loving, law-abiding citizens can be a fulfilling and honorable calling. Children will always need the security of boundaries set by loving parents under the guidance of God's Word.

We must teach our children that passive Christianity has no place in our world. If the people of God don't take action by praying for our country and our leaders, standing for what we know is right, and daring to voice our opposition to government practices that are clearly against God's Word, there will be no peace. As a parent, I want my children to learn that one person can make a difference and that even they can effect great change in their world.

In order for them to learn this principle, however, they must first see it at work in our lives. Each of us can do our part by writing letters to our political delegates, supporting pro-life and humanitarian organizations, and voting according to our Biblical convictions. And perhaps by setting the example for our children, they will do the same in their generation.

Dee Dee Wike

A MOTHER'S PRAYER

My prayer is not that you take them out of the world, but that you protect them from the evil one. They are not of the world, even as I am not of it. Sanctify them by the truth; your word is truth.

John 17:15–17

My children, especially my teenage son, have been the primary focus of my prayers lately. And these devotionals. Remembering what it was like to be fifteen with a thousand emotions creating chaos inside me, I feel his angst. In the true manner of a teenager, he thinks he can figure things out on his own and that his mom really doesn't know as much as she thinks she does. No matter how hard I try, I cannot convince him of the truths I have discovered the hard way. He is destined to discover those truths for himself by making mistakes, which could be avoided if he would simply listen.

I discovered one day, while reading the gospel of John, that Jesus actually prayed for his own children—us. In the seventeenth chapter of John's gospel, Jesus prays for his disciples and for all believers that God would protect them from the evil one, unite them in love and purpose, and bring them to live with him in glory. Jesus desired the Father's best for each of us—a life of abundant living, freedom from sin, and the joy of forever abiding in his presence.

As I think of and pray for my children, I want no less for them. I want them to grow up living joyfully as slaves to righteousness (Romans 6:18), not as slaves to sin and the culture in which they live. It is possible when we seek to follow God's ways and obey his Word to live above the level of mediocrity that pervades our worldly existence, to rise above the shackles of addictions and sin, and to soar on wings as eagles (Isaiah 40:31).

Don't we at times reject God's ways because we think our ways are better than his? Perhaps we don't take him at his word because we find his Word irrelevant for our day and age. Those of us who have tasted the sweetness of a life surrendered to God know that he truly knows what is best for his children. Let us set the example of obedience for our children by walking in obedience to our God.

Dee Dee Wike

I WANT TO LIVE

No, in all these things we are more than conquerors through him who loved us. For I am convinced that neither death nor life, neither angels nor demons, neither the present nor the future, nor any powers, neither height nor depth, nor anything else in all creation will be able to separate us from the love of God that is in Christ Jesus our Lord.

Romans 8:37–39

One of the things that has concerned me greatly is the amount of emotional baggage our kids are carrying these days. Their burdens are only made heavier by the heaps of garbage thrust upon them by their own peers. Add to that the influences of Facebook, MySpace, text messaging, and all manner of chemical substances, and you have a potentially deadly situation. Is it any wonder that our society is full of people, young and old, who are harming one another and themselves?

I grew up as a teenager in the seventies, the middle of six children, and life was hard even then. I can't imagine growing up as a teenager in the twenty-first century. Like so many of today's youth, I grew up with an identity crisis, feelings of loneliness and despair, and the feeling that anything would be better than living. When I see despondency in my own teenager, I try to reassure him and help him understand his value in God's eyes, and I pray like crazy.

Because my parents divorced when I was very young, I never really knew my birth father. My mom remarried before I turned two, so I grew up with a daddy; however, he traveled a lot in his work, leaving Mom to raise us pretty much by herself. Taught to respect my father and my stepdad, I always bought them Father's Day cards. To this day, I remember how difficult it was to stand in the card aisle and search for a card that expressed my love and honored them, while suppressing what my heart really felt—confusion, hurt, and abandonment. These feelings contributed to my own identity crisis.

Although I had received Christ as a young child and rededicated my life to him as a teenager, I didn't truly understand the depth of his love for me as a Father. Through my college and early career years, I struggled with feelings of rejection and tried desperately to find someone who could simply love and accept me for who I was. I began drinking to medicate the hurt and rejection and to fit in socially.

Although I was not necessarily unattractive physically, I found myself involved with people who were unattractive spiritually. The more involved I became with them, the more I began to loathe myself until I reached the point where death appeared to be my only hope of escaping the pain of living in a cruel world.

God, in his mercy, never left me during those years of searching. He never abandoned me when I turned my back on him and indulged in sinful, self-destructive living. As hard as I tried to destroy the person he created me to be, I could not. He would not allow it. He did allow me to hit rock bottom, however. He allowed me to become so desperate and hopeless that I reached for the only thing I knew to reach for—him. I knew that if I were to make it through my crisis and live to tell about it, then I would have to trust all I had been taught growing up. I would have to believe that God was who he said he was, that he was good, and that he loved me unconditionally, despite the wicked things I had done. I had to make a choice to forsake everything and everyone and follow him alone. I had to choose to live according to his truth, not the world's lies.

Once I laid hold of the truth that God loved me unconditionally and would be the Father that neither one of my earthly dads could be, I wanted to live. I wanted to make God proud of his daughter. I wanted to obey him because I finally knew that I could trust him to accept me as I was. I no longer felt I needed to change to please someone else because I was secure with my identity as a child of God.

How do we teach our kids these truths? How can we make sure they know who they are in Christ? We must first believe it for ourselves, live it out in front of them each day, and pray that God will reveal the truth to them in his perfect timing. We must pray for their protection on their own journey to discovering their true identity in Christ, and love them no matter what they do. These are hard things to do, but we must persevere and never give up. The minute we lose sight and give up the fight for our children is the minute we hand them over to the enemy who seeks to steal, kill, and destroy them.

Pray daily for your children to live abundant, fruitful lives for God's glory. The battle rages, the enemy is strong, but our God is victorious. The Lamb has overcome.

Dee Dee Wike

CHOICES MATTER

Now choose life, so that you and your children
may live and that you may love the LORD your
God, listen to his voice, and hold fast to him. For
the LORD is your life.

Deuteronomy 30:19–20

When God created man in his own image, he created us
with a free will, which enables us to make choices in life.
We are not puppets in the hands of a divine puppeteer
but rather men and women with the capability and intel-
ligence to make certain choices as we journey through life.

The Bible has much to say about making choices. We
can choose whom we serve (Joshua 24:15), how to spend
our time (Luke 10:42), and to pursue God's wisdom and
live according to his value system rather than the riches
and value system of our society (Proverbs 16:16). For
every choice we make, there is a reward or a consequence
(Galatians 6:7).

In parenting my children, I have talked with them often about the choices they make and the effects those choices will have on their young lives, both now and in the days to come. I know from experience that the choices I make directly affect my character and the image of Christ others may see in me. The same can be said of all of us. The choices we make in life really do matter.

Just as God gives us the free will to choose to do things, he also gives us the power of the Holy Spirit not to do things that are contrary to his will and to the Word of God. There is no addiction he can't deliver us from, no sin he can't forgive. I know, I've lived with addiction and committed sins too numerous to count. We all face temptation, but the Bible tells us, "No temptation has seized you except what is common to man. And God is faithful; he will not let you be tempted beyond what you can bear. But when you are tempted, he will also provide a way out so that you can stand up under it" (1 Corinthians 10:13). Here's the catch, though: we must choose to take the way out that God provides. God supplies the power to resist sin and temptation, but the choice to resist them is strictly up to us.

What choices will you make today? Ask God for wisdom to make the right choices and the courage to trust and obey Him in all things.

Dee Dee Wike

TRUTH WALKERS

I have no greater joy than to hear that my children are walking in the truth.

3 John 4

Some days when I read my Bible, a particular verse will stand out from the rest of the passage. Although the children referred to in this Scripture from the third epistle of John represent the Apostle John's spiritual offspring, this statement to his friend, Gaius, reflects the prayer of my own heart as a mother.

There are many Christian parents who long to see their children walking in the truth. Despite their best efforts to raise their children according to the principles set forth by God in his Word, they have watched their children, young and not-so-young, wander from the faith and the joy of an intimate relationship with the Lord. How does this happen? We make every effort to live our lives obediently and teach our children God's ways. How is it that even after they are saved, they turn away from a loving God and fall into sin? Some of the most God-fearing parents I know have prodigal children who have set aside God and his principles in favor of a more worldly and self-centered approach to life.

As a Baby Boomer, I grew up without so many of the influences that tug at the hearts and minds of my children today. We didn't hide behind Facebook, e-mail, text messaging, and voicemail. If we had something to say to someone, good or bad, we said it to his face or over the phone. Right was right, and wrong was wrong; there were very few gray areas in terms of sin and moral (or immoral) behavior. Sin was sin, and we often faced severe consequences for our wrongdoing.

With so many worldly influences working against us today, it has become increasingly difficult for parents to teach their children, and for children to learn, what it means to have a truly committed walk with the Lord and to obey his Word. There are no guaranties that even if we do everything right, parenting our children according to God's Word, they will journey through this life without making some major and potentially devastating mistakes.

The heartbreak in parenting our children, at least for me, comes from seeing them make needless mistakes, which can have far-reaching and long-lasting consequences. When we have made our mistakes and learned from them, we want so badly to prevent our children from doing the same. We want them to mature quickly in their walk with God, bypassing the trouble that they will have in this world and settling into a victorious and intimate relationship with him. Seldom does life work that way.

So what can we do? How do we face the challenges and heartbreak of parenting our twenty-first-century children with the confidence that they will turn out okay in the end? First, we must pray without ceasing for our children and ourselves, as their parents.

Then, we must set the example for them, living holy lives without compromising the principles of God's Word. We must exhibit the kind of faith we desire for them to have, the kind of faith they must have in order to survive the journey. Finally, we must hold on to the promise that if we "train a child in the way he should go, when he is old he will not turn from it" (Proverbs 22:6). That doesn't mean he won't stray; I did. But if we lay the foundation, loving and nurturing our children in the ways of God, there is a far greater chance that they will eventually find their way back home to the Father.

THE DUCK FAMILY

He will cover you with his feathers, and under his
wings you will find refuge; his faithfulness will be
your shield and rampart.

Psalm 91:4

As my son and I were leaving his music lesson, he called
my attention to a mama duck and her fourteen ducklings.
Although tiny and only a day or two old, they closely followed their mama as she led them in and out of the protection of some shrubs near the spot where I had parked
the car. Because my mind was on tackling the next thing
on my to-do list, I didn't even notice these precious crea-
tures. How thankful I am that my son wasn't too preoc-
cupied with his own agenda to see them.

Regrettably, I had left home without my camera and had
only my cell phone with which to take pictures. Knowing
that my phone's camera wouldn't do justice to our discov-

Dee Dee Wike

ery, we drove home to pick up my digital camera and my daughter, and then we returned to the site where we saw the ducks, hoping that they would still be there. It took several minutes of searching for them, but we finally found them on the pond of a nearby retirement center.

As we watched this family of mallards, God impressed upon me some truths that I was able to share with my children.

First, just as the mama duck did her brood, he covers us with his feathers and hides us under his wings, sheltering and protecting us from the dangers of living in this world (Psalm 91:4–9). Although we initially only saw one duckling with its mother, there were actually fourteen hiding beneath the wings. Only when she stood could we see them all. God's wings are large enough to cover all his children.

Secondly, as we draw near to God through prayer and obey his commands to us in the Scriptures, we become more like him. As the mama and daddy ducks communicated with each other and with their ducklings, the babies were swift to obey and follow their mama, trusting that she and Daddy knew best and would keep them safe.

Last, as we watched them and listened to them communicate with each other, we witnessed an amazing sight. The mama duck waddled to the water, jumped in, and swam across the pond to where the daddy stood, knowing her ducklings would find safety if they chose to follow her. The little ones instinctively obeyed her call, jumping into the water for what may have been their first swim. When they got to the opposite shore, each one struggled to make it up the slippery shoreline and onto dry ground. Not one duckling made it out of the water on the first attempt, but each persevered with the encouragement of their parents and siblings until they managed to find safety on the other shore.

The dependence of these ducklings upon their parents to guide and keep them safe so clearly illustrated for me the need we all have for God's loving guidance and care. My children and I were no real threat, but the little ducklings didn't know that. They huddled together, encouraged each other, and obeyed the commands of the loving parents whom they trusted to keep them safe. God is no less a loving parent; in fact, he has proven over and over to me that Father truly does know best.

Dee Dee Wike

LEARNING
TO LISTEN

My sheep listen to my voice; I know them and
they follow me.

John 10:27

Each morning, I have a quiet time when I meet with the
Lord, read his Word, and pray. If you were to read my
journal, though, you would find that my conversations
with God are very one-sided. That is because I haven't yet
mastered the art of listening to God, although I am quite
adept at talking to him. He longs to hear the voices of his
children and listen to our concerns, but he longs to speak
to us as well. When I sit down, open my Bible, and take
up my pen, it's usually so I can tell him every little detail

and need of my life. Rarely do I stop long enough for God to get a word in edgewise.

With all the distractions and to-do lists in our lives, how do we quiet ourselves long enough to hear the voice of God? Like Martha, my mind tends to think about all I have to do in the hours before me, not focus on what the Lord might be saying to me in my quiet time. I sometimes struggle to let go of my daily concerns so that I can receive the deeper things of God.

Although I am a big proponent of journaling and find it helpful in keeping my prayer life focused, sometimes the practice becomes more of a distraction than a spiritual discipline. Some days I need to lay down the pen, be still, and know that God is God. It isn't necessary to continually remind him of my needs; he knows already, and he will not forget.

A few years ago, my son taught me a lesson I will never forget. As we were praying on our way to school, he ended his prayer with this statement: "Lord, I hope *you* have a good day." His prayer made me stop and question how often I pray for God to be blessed instead of asking that he bless me. So often when I pray, my focus is usually on the needs of others or myself, not on God's greatness or how I can be a blessing to him.

If we want to grow in our relationship with God, we must learn to listen. He has so much he wants to tell us, but he can't get through to us if we don't quiet ourselves and listen for his still, small voice.

Dee Dee Wike

A MATTER OF PERSPECTIVE

Each of you should look not only to your own interests, but also to the interests of others.

Philippians 2:4

During my quiet time, I often ponder the lessons I learned from the previous day in order to come up with a devotional to write and share with others. However, not every day stands out; not every life experience carries a lesson for me. Some days are just ordinary, yet each day is challenging in some way.

Some challenges are ordinary too. While I feel the financial strain of living in a recession and wonder when I'll ever pay off the mountain of debt I owe, this problem is not unique to me; it is something many of us deal with daily. Though annoying, money matters are not my greatest concern; God has promised to take care of our daily needs, and he has remained faithful to that promise. I may not have everything I want, but I have everything I need because of his gracious provision.

Some challenges, however, are more difficult than others. Whether the hurt over a friendship that has changed, the frustration of dealing with an adolescent who sees no value in education or the concern over family and friends with cancer and chronic illnesses, matters involving my heart and the people I love are burdensome and hard to bear.

When I consider my problems, I am reminded that they are minuscule in light of eternity and in comparison with what others deal with every day. For instance, my son, though strong-willed and unmotivated, doesn't have a life-threatening illness. I know of a parent whose teenage son has been battling cancer and has just received a grim prognosis. News of this most recent development certainly puts my problems in perspective.

Praying for and considering the need of others is a great antidote to self-pity and worry over our own problems. Giving what we possess, whether money, time, or talent, is a great way to take our minds off our own problems and make a difference in the life of someone else.

As you mull over your troubles today, consider the lives of the people around you. What challenges are they facing? How can you help shoulder their burden and lighten their load? As you lay aside your own problems to shoulder the burden of a fellow human being, your perspective will change, and you may find that your load is not as heavy as you thought.

Dee Dee Wike

LOSING AMERICA

"Don't be afraid," the prophet answered. "Those who are with us are more than those who are with them." And Elisha prayed, "O Lord, open his eyes so he may see."

2 Kings 6:16–17a

After reading the local and national headlines one morning, my heart was broken over the clear and very disturbing realization that we're losing America and any hope our children may have of living the American dream in a peaceful, prosperous nation.

When schools are instituting programs to teach kindergartners foreign languages, abortion is legalized, illegal drug use is glorified, laws are introduced to strip parents of their rights to raise and educate their children, and all efforts are made to remove the influence of Christianity in our society, it is clear that things have changed and not for the better. Where do we draw the line between tolerance and political correctness and the blatant disregard for the biblical principles on which our nation was founded?

The America of today is not the America I grew up in. People are no longer willing to fight for the values and principles that made our nation a place of great freedom and opportunity. Patriotism and peaceful activism have been replaced with a determined effort to destroy any remnant of moral decency and political democracy.

Who are the ones who will fight to win America back? In Isaiah 6:8, the prophet Isaiah says, "Then I heard the voice of the Lord saying, 'Whom shall I send? And who will go for us?' And I said, 'Here am I. Send me!'" I believe God is crying out today for Christians and patriots to rise up and reclaim the America we once knew.

Is it too late to save our beloved nation? Have we passed the point of no return? The last verses of Isaiah chapter six give me hope that it is not too late. Although these are the words of the Lord spoken to Isaiah regarding the nation of Israel, they are my prayer for America today: "And though a tenth remains in the land, it will again be laid waste. But as the terebinth and oak leave stumps when they are cut down, so the holy seed will be the stump in the land" (v. 13). I believe that it is not too late for God to save America, but he needs soldiers who are willing to take up their shield of faith and the sword of the Spirit and fight in his behalf.

Will you go? Will you fight to reclaim our great nation?

OUCH! THAT HURTS!

Teach me your way, O LORD, and I will walk in your truth; give me an undivided heart, that I may fear your name. I will praise you, O Lord my God, with all my heart; I will glorify your name forever.

Psalm 86:11–12

As much as we hate to admit it, we love the things we possess so much that letting go of them becomes nearly impossible. The thing we cherish could be material, like our first car, or relational, like our first love or a friendship that becomes dear to us. Yet there comes a time when we must let go of that which steals our affection from God. We must lay down our idols because God demands it: "You shall have no other gods before me" (Exodus 20:3).

Letting go is something I struggle with daily. Whether it is my side of an argument or some earthly treasure, I sometimes find my fingers so tightly clutched around the object of my affections that the pain is excruciating when God begins to pry my fingers loose. Often the pain is not felt in my hands but in my heart. I reach a place of brokenness that causes me to cry out for God's mercy and grace.

What is the thing that you are holding on to for dear life? If it is anything other than Jesus, then you are holding on to an idol and loving God with a divided heart. When you fail to surrender every area of your life to the Lordship of Christ, you hinder his purpose and plan for you. Because God loves and desires intimate fellowship with his children, he will do whatever it takes to remove anything—material or relational—that stands between us and him, no matter how painful the process or how long it takes. We would be wise to hold loosely the things of this world and hold tightly to him. No person can love us like Jesus can, and no material thing can satisfy the deep longings of our heart.

Dee Dee Wike

STRUGGLING WITH MOTIVES

All a man's ways seem innocent to him, but motives are weighed by the LORD.

Proverbs 16:2

Several weeks ago, I made the decision to take a leave of absence from the choir at our church in order to audit a lay counselor training class. It seemed a good idea at the time, and indeed, the class has provided beneficial information I can use as I deal with relational issues and prepare for whatever service God may require of me. Weeks into the course, however, I find myself struggling with, yet resisting, the desire to return to choir. It is a complicated issue for me.

Realizing that my decision whether or not to return to choir has more to do with my own personal agenda than worshipping God and serving the body of Christ, I have confessed my motivational dilemma to him. As I seek to understand my own heart and mind on the matter, I know that until my heart is aligned with his will I must remain on the sidelines.

Life presents us with opportunities every day, which require prayerful consideration and wise decision-making. In everything we do, our motives should be to worship God, be obedient to his will for us, and glorify him. But often we find ourselves, or at least I do, questioning the purity of our motives.

What is it that motivates you? Is it money, power, or the desire for man's approval? Today, pray for God to show you his heart on the matter. I, for one, would rather glorify God in one act of service than gain man's approval in ten.

PLEASE, PLEASE WAIT A MINUTE, MR. POSTMAN

Every good and perfect gift is from above, coming down from the Father of the heavenly lights, who does not change like shifting shadows.

James 1:17

For years, the poodle has been recognized as a highly intelligent dog breed. But what some people may not know is that poodles can also be quite amusing, often without meaning to be. Despite the expense of grooming and medical care, they are a great source of joy for those who are fortunate enough to own one.

My poodle, Madison, is very smart and lately has begun barking at every mail truck she sees as if to say, "Over here! I'm over here!" That's because our postal carrier, Charlie, has made it his practice to give her dog biscuits every time we happen to meet him at the mailbox. He has even been known to leave a dog biscuit for Madison and candy for my children on the stack of mail he places in the mailbox when we are not there. Now every time Madison sees a mail truck, she just assumes that Charlie is driving it.

Just this afternoon, the mail truck pulled up to the neighbor's mailbox, and Madison started barking and moving toward the truck. I wish you could have seen the look of hurt and confusion on her face when the truck, driven by a substitute mail carrier, passed her by. Her pleading bark quickly turned to fussing as the mail carrier pulled away from the mailbox without giving her a dog biscuit.

Thankfully, God is never off-duty with a substitute filling in for him. When we call to him, he answers and gives us everything we need in his perfect timing. Maybe not everything we want, but certainly everything we need. As smart as Madison is, she doesn't understand why the mail carrier didn't give her a dog biscuit as she expected. However, I know that when God doesn't give me what I ask for, he knows that it's not in my best interest *and* it probably isn't something I really need in the first place. He is faithful to give me his best and never requires me to settle for anything less.

NOTHING TO FEAR

I sought the LORD, and he answered me; he
delivered me from all my fears.

Psalm 34:4

I know a lot of people who do not watch the news because
hardly is there ever good news. There are some who hear
bad news reports and lose all ability to think rationally
about what may never even touch them. Why are people
so fearful? Maybe it's because they don't know our God.

The God I know is a loving God. He doesn't go
around zapping humanity with every ailment and adversity known to man. Some things we simply bring on ourselves because we fail to do the things we know we ought
to do. No one asked for swine flu to become a pandemic;
the media did an outstanding job of making it yet another
cause for global concern. We were reminded of the com-
monsense measures that we could take to help insure that

we did not contract the virus, such as covering our mouths and noses when we sneeze or cough, staying away from people who are sick, and washing our hands—all those things our mothers taught us to do.

The God I know is a sovereign God. Because he is sovereign, I need not fear anything. The Bible tells me that he is my refuge and strength and my source of protection, provision, and healing. Because I know God and believe that his Word is true, "even though I walk through the valley of the shadow of death, I will fear no evil, for you are with me; your rod and your staff, they comfort me" (Psalm 23:4).

If you are afraid of anything, I encourage you to take to heart these words of assurance from Psalm 91:

> He who dwells in the shelter of the Most High will rest in the shadow of the Almighty. I will say of the LORD, "He is my refuge and my fortress, my God, in whom I trust." Surely he will save you from the fowler's snare and from the deadly pestilence. He will cover you with his feathers, and under his wings you will find refuge; his faithfulness will be your shield and rampart. You will not fear the terror of night, nor the arrow that flies by day, nor the pestilence that stalks in the darkness, nor the plague that destroys at midday. A thousand may fall at your side, ten thousand at your right hand, but it will not come near you.
>
> Psalm 91:1–7

Someone once defined fear as False Evidence Appearing Real. What is your reality today? Are you trusting in the one true God?

Dee Dee Wike

SUNDAY IS COMING

The Lord is not slow in keeping his promise, as some understand slowness. He is patient with you, not wanting anyone to perish, but everyone to come to repentance.

2 Peter 3:9

 The longer I live, and the more I grow in my relationship with Jesus, the more I appreciate the significance of his sacrificial death for my sins. As I reflect on his life and all that occurred on that first Good Friday, I rejoice because I know that Sunday came soon after, and Jesus rose from the dead, forever eradicating the death penalty for my sins and instilling the hope and promise of intimate fellowship with him.

As Christians, we often find ourselves discouraged or disheartened because of our loved ones—friends, wayward children, other family members—who remain separated from God because of their sin and rebellion. Despite all our efforts to convince them that life in Christ is a life of abundance and joy, they are determined to live life apart from him, forfeiting the joy of receiving his best for them. We pray and plead with God to change them when perhaps what we really need is for God to change us.

It is not God's will that we should be discouraged or disheartened but rather determined to prevail in prayer for them and to boldly claim the promises of his Word. At one time, we were all prodigals. Many of us can recall the depravity of our own sin, and the very day that Jesus lifted us out of the mud and mire and set our feet upon a rock, giving us a firm place to stand (Psalm 40:2). We know that Christ died for us while we were yet sinners (Romans 5:8). How can we not believe that he will do the same for our wayward children, our lost friends, and our family members who have not experienced his salvation or the power of his resurrection?

Have faith, dear ones. Sunday came for you. Believe that by virtue of God's Word, his promises, and the sacrifice of his dear Son, it will come for your loved one as well. You may have to pray for a very long time for your prodigal to turn back to God or discover him for the very first time, but keep watching the horizon. Never give up hope. God never gave up on you.

A MELANCHOLY EASTER

On the evening of that first day of the week, when the disciples were together, with the doors locked for fear of the Jews, Jesus came and stood among them and said, "Peace be with you!" After he said this, he showed them his hands and side. The disciples were overjoyed when they saw the Lord.

John 20:19–20

Easter is supposed to be a time of joyous celebration of our Savior's resurrection, but one year I found myself dealing with a mixed bag of emotions. The days leading up to Easter were ones of quiet reflection of what Christ did for me on the cross. As I thought about his sacrifice, thoughts of sorrow that my sin resulted in his death were mixed with intense gratitude for his amazing love and willing sacrifice. Intermingled in all those thoughts were fond memories of Easters past and a longing to spend this holiday with my family, who are now scattered across the country. What sweet times those were.

I suppose there are many people who felt a little melancholy this Easter. Perhaps you were one of them. Whether you suffered the loss of a loved one this year, or your Easter was clouded by illness or the stress of dealing with unpleasant family or financial issues, Easter might have seemed like just another day. As hard as I tried to make this a special day for my own family, in many ways it was just another Sunday.

Those who followed Christ were surely faced with their own mixed emotions following his crucifixion. Memories of Christ's teachings, his healing, his compassion, and even his humor were no doubt mingled with fear, regret, and unbearable sadness. Because of disbelief and disillusionment over the death of their Messiah and the deep sorrow they felt over their loss, hope seemed impossible until the impossible occurred. How quickly their despair turned to triumphant joy when the resurrected Lord "stood among them and said, 'Peace be with you!' The disciples were overjoyed when they saw the Lord" (John 20:19–20).

So it should be with us. No matter how melancholy we may feel at times because of our circumstances, our memories, and our disappointments, we must remember that the resurrected Lord is standing among us and be overjoyed at his daily presence in our lives.

WASHED OUT,
NOT WASHED UP

But we have this treasure in jars of clay to show that this all-surpassing power is from God and not from us. We are hard pressed on every side, but not crushed; perplexed, but not in despair; persecuted, but not abandoned; struck down, but not destroyed.

2 Corinthians 4:7–9

Don't you hate it when you plan a weekend of fun outdoor activities and the weather doesn't cooperate? Quite often, especially in the spring, clouds darken, and the skies pour buckets of rain when we least expect it, resulting in a total washout.

Life isn't fair. Sometimes we face challenges we didn't ask for, such as the death of a loved one or the loss of a job. The stresses of life can become overwhelming, yet God offers us his strength and the wisdom of his Word to weather the storms we encounter on our journey.

When you feel overwhelmed by your own challenges, rather than focus on the problems and the odds stacked against you, turn to God's Word and confess with your mouth all you know to be true about God's character. Money is tight, but God's Word assures you that God will supply all your daily needs. You may suffer rejection by well-meaning friends and family, but you can have the assurance that your loving heavenly Father will never reject you. When you feel as if everyone has deserted you to cope with circumstances on your own, remember that God has promised never to leave you or forsake you. With God, you may be washed out, but you are never washed up. He is bigger than any problem, more faithful than anyone you know, and able to do abundantly more than you can ask or imagine.

Dee Dee Wike

POSITIONED TO PRAISE GOD

Then Job stood up, tore his robe and shaved his head. He fell to the ground and worshiped, saying: "Naked I came from my mother's womb, and naked I will leave this life. The LORD gives, and the LORD takes away. Praise the name of the LORD." Throughout all this Job did not sin or blame God for anything.

Job 1:20–22, HCSB

Many of us are born complainers. We fuss about every little thing that happens to us, often blaming others, perhaps even God, for our misfortune and adversity. As we lament our negative circumstances, not only do we reinforce them in our own mind, but we subject others to our negative attitudes as well. I try not to be an "air polluter," but sometimes I am guilty of focusing on and confessing the more challenging aspects of daily life rather than praising God for what he wants to teach me through them.

Job, a man known to have suffered greatly, was not like that. In the first chapter of Job, we are told that in a very short time, he lost everything he held dear: his livestock, his home, his servants, his children, and even his health. Only his nagging wife remained, and she wasn't much help. Yet despite all the loss he suffered, Job still managed to praise God.

Recently, God revealed to me that sometimes true worship comes when we are left with nothing except him. That's where Job finds himself in this passage, naked as the day he was born and stripped of all he held dear. "Then Job stood up, tore his robe and shaved his head. He fell to the ground and worshiped" (Job 1:20).

Notice Job's posture of praise. He worshiped God from the lowest possible position—the ground. He humbled himself under the hand of his almighty, sovereign Lord and worshiped him, despite all the loss he had suffered. He acknowledged that all he had lost had been given to him by God in the first place and that God had the right to take it away if he so desired. Job never complained, not even to his nagging wife, that God was unjust or that life was unfair. Rather Job accepted the good with the bad and praised God anyway because he knew that worshipping God was not dependent on what he owned, but on the one who owned him.

What is it that keeps you from praising God today? A broken relationship, a wayward child, an addiction that you just can't seem to break? Rather than blame God, fall on your face and worship him. Mourn if you must;

Job certainly did. Pour out your heart to God and praise him for his sovereignty. Ask him to show you the purpose behind all that troubles you and surrender yourself to his will. When you have hit rock bottom, remember the words of Betsy Ten Boom: "There is no pit so deep that God is not deeper still."

ALL SHOOK UP

I have set the LORD always before me. Because he
is at my right hand, I will not be shaken.

Psalm 16:8

Life in my household is never dull nor boring. It seems
that when God is not shaking things up, the devil is.

Our first year of homeschool was anything but a walk
in the park. Not only were we new to the journey, but
added to the mix were the wild and crazy hormones of
adolescence, which caused my strong-willed teenager to
assert his independent thinking in some unanticipated
ways. After months of battling a lack of motivation, my
son was determined that he would finish the school year
after all, which meant that we would all have to scramble
in order to make it happen.

Discouragement is no stranger to us. Sometimes he
walks in unexpectedly; at other times, his presence is a

Dee Dee Wike

constant undercurrent in our daily lives. No matter how discouraged we become, however, we need not be shaken. God's Word gives us encouragement to keep putting one foot in front of the other.

"He alone is my rock and my salvation; he is my fortress, I will never be shaken" (Psalm 62:2).

"Surely he will never be shaken; a righteous man will be remembered forever. His heart is secure, he will have no fear; in the end he will triumph over his foes" (Psalm 112:6–7).

"'Though the mountains be shaken and the hills removed, yet my unfailing love for you will not be shaken nor my covenant of peace be removed,' says the LORD, who has compassion on you" (Isaiah 54:10).

Are you discouraged today? Know that God is in control of your circumstances and that he sees everything you cannot see. He knows the outcome. He has a plan, a good plan to prosper and not harm you, to give you a hope and a future (Jeremiah 29:11).

MATTERS OF THE HEART

For great is your love, higher than the heavens;
your faithfulness reaches to the skies.

Psalm 108:4

If love is a many splendored thing, then why are hearts so easily broken? How can true and sincere love for another human being erode into apathy and disappointment?

God is love, and he gave human beings a great capacity to love one another. While his love for us is unconditional and limitless, as humans, we are incapable of extending that kind of love to one another. Sadly, we expect others to love us as perfectly as God does, and when they don't, we become disillusioned, disappointed, and heartbroken.

Dee Dee Wike

God commands that we love him above all others and not make idols of anything or any person. Yet many of us put those we love on a pedestal, exerting more effort to nurture our relationships with one another than our relationship with God. Our love becomes unbalanced, and the pedestal topples, leaving brokenness in its wake.

Matters of the heart are tricky, and a lonely heart is defenseless against sin's subtle approach. A fleeting glance, a kind remark, and a gentle touch are sometimes all it takes to tarnish the pure love God intended us to have for one another and lure us into a relationship that is not within God's will. We flirt not only with the one who captures our heart but with sin itself, coming dangerously close to blurring the lines and overstepping the boundaries that God has set for us in his Word.

Christians are not exempt from the temptation to be unfaithful, but we can resist it if we are walking closely enough with God to fall under the conviction of his Holy Spirit and turn away from any relationship that would cause us to sin. When we make our relationship with God our first priority, loving him above all others and obeying what he has commanded in his Word, then he will satisfy us with his love.

If you find yourself in a relationship that you know is outside the will of God, walk away from it today and run into the arms of the true and faithful one. Jesus has said,

As the Father has loved me, so have I loved you.
Now remain in my love. If you obey my commands,
you will remain in my love, just as I have obeyed

my Father's commands and remain in his love. I
have told you this so that my joy may be in you and
that your joy may be complete.

John 15:9–12

Dee Dee Wike

TOMORROW MAY NEVER COME

Why, you do not even know what will happen
tomorrow. What is your life? You are a mist that
appears for a little while and then vanishes.

James 4:14

I recently received word that a friend's twenty-six-year-
old son had been tragically killed in a car accident. As I
read the ages of people listed in the obituary section of
our newspaper, I realized that my opportunity to make
a difference in this world is quickly passing and that my
life could be gone in an instant. Without the guarantee
that tomorrow will come for any of us, we need a renewed
sense of urgency to live life fully today.

What is the dream you long to see fulfilled? What things are you doing to make a difference in the lives of the people around you? What obstacles are keeping you from making bold steps toward accomplishing the goals you have set for yourself?

The Bible tells us, "Do not boast about tomorrow, for you do not know what a day may bring forth" (Proverbs 27:1). We are quick to brag about the great things we plan to do someday yet put off working toward our goals, thinking that we have all the time in the world to achieve them.

We cannot wait until tomorrow to begin making a difference in the lives of the people around us—they, or we, may not live that long. We cannot wait until everything is perfectly aligned to do what God has called us to do. Life is messy, and conditions will never be perfect, but God can work through us in spite of any obstacles we may face.

The most important thing I can do today is love those around me. If God takes me home tomorrow, I want my family to know how much I loved them today. If my husband or one of my children is suddenly taken from me, I want the peace of knowing that my last words to them were words of love, not rebuke.

Chris Tomlin is a brilliant songwriter and penned the following words:

I want to live like there's no tomorrow
I want to dance like no one's around
I want to sing like nobody's listening
Before I lay my body down
I want to give like I have plenty
I want to love like I'm not afraid
I want to be the man I was meant to be
I want to be the way I was made.

Today, live like there is no tomorrow. Be the way God made you. Touch another human's soul and make a difference in your world.

BECOMING MY MOTHER

Her children arise and call her blessed; her husband also, and he praises her: "Many women do noble things, but you surpass them all. Charm is deceptive, and beauty is fleeting; but a woman who fears the LORD is to be praised."

Proverbs 31:28–30

It is not uncommon for women to look in the mirror and say, "I'm becoming my mother!" There is something profoundly mysterious in the way that we begin to take on the resemblance and personality traits of our parents as we mature.

Every time someone tells me how much I look like my mother, I receive that as a compliment. Truly, Mom is a beautiful woman. But more than anything, I want

Dee Dee Wike

my heart to be as beautiful as hers—the heart of a loving and generous woman who sees the needs of others as far greater than her own.

What individual has had the most profound influence on your life? Perhaps your parents are your positive role model, or maybe you grew up looking for love and guidance from a teacher, Scout leader, or youth minister at church. Each of us has an individual we admire, a person we aspire to emulate in some way or other.

For the Christian, Jesus is the ultimate role model. As we study scripture to learn of him, we see that he was the embodiment of godliness, truth, grace, and mercy. Is it possible for us to model our lives after his and have the kind of impact on others that Jesus did? Not in our own strength. However, the Holy Spirit us enables us to grow in our knowledge of God and live our lives in such a way that others see him in us.

As much as I aspire to be a godly woman like my mother, even more I desire to reflect the glory and exhibit the character of the loving God who lives inside me. As we spend time in the presence of our heavenly Father each day, before long people will look and say, "He's becoming his Father."

SOLACE IN OUR SUFFERING

Surely he took up our infirmities and carried our
sorrows, yet we considered him stricken by God,
smitten by him and afflicted. But he was pierced
for our transgressions, he was crushed for our
iniquities; the punishment that brought us peace
was upon him, and by his wounds we are healed.

Isaiah 53:4–5

Not a day goes by that I don't consider how stressful life
has become, not just for me, but for everyone I know. We
are living like hamsters on an exercise wheel, frantically
running but seemingly getting nowhere. Always taking
three steps forward and two steps back, we barely keep
our heads above water and make painfully slow progress,
if any, toward our goals. We are often distracted from
things that are important by activities and attitudes that

are counterproductive. Frustration becomes a vicious enemy that takes its toll on our energy and fruitfulness.

Perhaps the most difficult circumstances we deal with are those that involve the people closest to us. We worry about loved ones who are not saved or walking with the Lord or who are suffering the ravages of addiction, financial reversal, or the loss of someone close to them. We have to interact daily with people who may not see life the way we do, who are self-centered and irritating, and who need a whole lot of grace and patience. Quite frankly, we grow weary at times and long for the day when we will leave this troubled earth and enter into eternal fellowship and worship in the presence of our Lord.

This dilemma of suffering is not unique to us. Jesus himself had to deal with many of the same issues we do today. When we are brokenhearted over a relationship or weary of dealing with the daily struggles of life, we have only to look to God's Word to see that Jesus probably felt the same way we do. After all, although he was fully God, he was also fully human and subject to the same temptations and sorrows that we face. Even as he prayed, "Father, if you are willing, take this cup from me; yet not my will, but yours be done" (Luke 22:42), he knew that even the best life on earth could not compare with the peace and glory of the heaven he left in order to come live among us.

As difficult and demanding as our lives and our service for Christ may be, if we do not grow weary in doing good, we shall reap a harvest if we do not give up (Galatians 6:9). Like the apostle Paul, we will be able to say with conviction,

I have fought the good fight, I have finished the race, I have kept the faith. Now there is in store for me the crown of righteousness, which the Lord, the righteous Judge, will award to me on that day—and not only to me, but also to all who have longed for his appearing.

2 Timothy 4:8

JUST ANOTHER DAY

> She gets up while it is still dark; she provides food for her family and portions for her servant girls. She considers a field and buys it; out of her earnings she plants a vineyard. She sets about her work vigorously; her arms are strong for her tasks...She watches over the affairs of her household and does not eat the bread of idleness.
>
> Proverbs 31:15–17, 27

Mother's Day is just another day for many women. Even though we may go out to lunch after church and receive the customary cards and gifts from our families, there is still laundry to do, two other meals to be considered, and a pervading sense of normalcy that is a part of everyday life. Such is the life of a mother.

Despite the mundane tasks of motherhood, on Mother's Day I did manage to squeeze in a brief nap and was thoroughly entertained by my daughter, who wrote, directed, and acted out a very creative puppet show. She can be quite amusing. My son wrote an ever-so-sweet note to me in the steam on the bathroom mirror, and my husband baked some delicious chocolate chip cookies and cleaned up the mess. The day was not without its blessings, but it was indeed just another day.

You see, the beautiful part of being a mother in my household is that my kids and my spouse often surprise me with little gifts of love. Not a day goes by that I don't thank God for them. Life is not all rosy; we certainly have our share of challenges, chores, and squabbles. But we share a strong foundation of love that covers our shortcomings and a common faith that gives us the strength and determination to walk through life together day after day.

According to the calendar, Mother's Day comes once a year. But for the woman of God who cherishes her family and her role as a mom, every day is Mother's Day. Whether you have little ones at home, grown ones far away, or have been a spiritual mother to one of God's own special children, may you find joy in the noble calling God has placed on your life.

IN IT TOGETHER

For you, O God, tested us; you refined us like silver. You brought us into prison and laid burdens on our backs. You let men ride over our heads; we went through fire and water, but you brought us to a place of abundance.

Psalm 66:10–12

Lately, life has seemed like more of a rat race than a reason to rejoice. In the midst of all the activity, I have somehow become focused on everything that is wrong rather than on the one who can make all things right. I have forgotten that as difficult and unpleasant as circumstances may be at times, God has ordained every one of my days and has tailored every test and trial to refine me into a vessel of honor, "useful to the Master and prepared to do any good work" (2 Timothy 2:21).

When you read Psalm 66:10–12, what do you see? How often do we blame others for our adversities when Scripture plainly tells us that it is God who has tested us? He is refining us like silver, a process that requires fire and intense heat in order to craft a quality vessel. Do you sometimes feel like your life is a prison and your back is breaking under the heavy burden you carry? We are told God has "brought us into prison and laid burdens on our backs." Do you feel like the human race has run you over? These verses tell us that God "let men ride over our heads." We may feel there is no end to the fire and water through which we go every day, but we don't go through them alone. In Isaiah 43:2–3, God declares:

> When you pass through the waters, I will be with you; and when you pass through the rivers, they will not sweep over you. When you walk through the fire, you will not be burned; the flames will not set you ablaze. For I am the Lord, your God, the Holy One of Israel, your Savior.

God is with us in everything we do and every challenge we face. The beauty of these promises from God's Word is not only the blessed assurance that God himself is with us but that when all is said and done he will bring us to a "place of abundance."

SIMPLY TRUST

The LORD will fight for you; you need only to be still.

Exodus 14:14

Intense struggles often elicit fervent prayer from God's people, and that is how it should be. But like a dieter so obsessed with what she shouldn't eat that she thinks about food constantly, we become so focused on our problems when praying that we never truly release them to God's care. Rather than remember that our work is to pray and let go so God can do his work, our tendency is to hold on and try to help God fix the things that only he can fix.

Jesus said, "And when you pray, do not keep on babbling like pagans, for they think they will be heard because of their many words. Do not be like them, for your Father knows what you need before you ask him" (Matthew 6:7–8). In other words, pray and release, let go and let God. He is able. If we could only grasp that truth and trust God to complete the good work he has begun not only in our lives but in the lives of those loved ones who so desperately need him, then we might actually experience the peace and joy God desires for us to walk in.

Simply Trust

It matters not how oft I pray
Or cares upon you thrust.
Just for today, I choose to sit,
Be still, and simply trust.

No matter how hard I pray, the world
Will turn, as well it must.
Just for today, I choose to sit,
Be still, and simply trust.

Because I know that You alone
Are faithful, true, and just,
Abiding in Your matchless love, I will
Be still, and simply trust.

Dee Dee Wike

WAKE-UP CALL

For to me, living means living for Christ, and dying is even better. But if I live, I can do more fruitful work for Christ. So I really don't know which is better. I'm torn between two desires: I long to go and be with Christ, which would be far better for me. But for your sakes, it is better that I continue to live.

Philippians 1:21–24, NLT

Driving home from a bridal shower on a beautiful Sunday afternoon, I was thinking of taking a long walk when my cell phone rang. On the other end was a friend calling to let me know her son had been rushed to the hospital. Hearing the fear in her voice, I immediately drove to the hospital to be with her as she waited to see if he would pull through. Seeing him in the intensive care unit hooked up to a ventilator and fighting for his life was a wake-up call for me.

There are times when life takes an unexpected turn and we find ourselves in a pit of despair. Or, we cave into the stresses of life wishing for anything that might bring relief from the pain of disappointment and heartbreak. There are many people, even in our churches, who appear okay on the outside but are waging their own secret war against depression, despair, and anxiety. The enemy seeks to steal our joy, kill our spirit, and destroy our witness anyway he can, and quite often we are no match for his tactics. But God is.

Daily we must remind ourselves that God is with us in every situation, whether good or bad. Even though we may not enjoy life some days, we can rest assured that God is in control of even our most challenging circumstances and that he will give us the strength we need to persevere through them.

As believers we will one day live in heaven where there is no sorrow, suffering, or hopelessness. As much as we may look forward to that day, it is not up to us to usher in that day ahead of God's schedule. God has a purpose for each of us and work for us to do during our allotted time on this earth. Though we may long to be with Christ, it is important that we remain here to encourage others who are struggling in their journey and to introduce Christ to those who don't know him.

I don't know the challenges you face that make life seem unbearable. Know this, though: God is with you, he understands your pain, and he desires for you to lay your burdens at his feet. His shoulders are broad enough to carry your heavy load, his arms are strong enough to carry

Dee Dee Wike

you when you are too weary to walk another step, and his grace is sufficient for every need you have. Call on Jesus today. He loves you and will be your refuge, your strength, and a very present help in time of need.

GROWING UP
TOO FAST

But grow in the grace and knowledge of our Lord
and Savior Jesus Christ.

2 Peter 3:18

In our society, children grow up way too fast. Between the cultural influences that are thrust at them early on and the adult behaviors they often have to assume at an early age because of family circumstances, their innocence and the fine art of simply being a child are lost. How I wish my children could grow up as I did, enjoying simple pleasures, face-to-face conversations with friends, and exploring their world experientially rather than through a computer screen!

I am blessed to have great children who, in their own right, are creative, imaginative, and full of surprises. Last night, my daughter dressed up and prepared a handwritten invitation to a private Hawaiian party in the backyard. Tucking a rose behind my ear, she had me close my eyes and led me to the backyard, where she had set up lawn chairs, an umbrella, and a bucket of "ocean water" to soak my feet in.

Granted, it was a little chilly but, eager to please, she went inside and got a bowl of hot water to take off the chill so I would leave my feet in the bucket longer than two seconds. Another trip inside the house yielded a delicious home-baked cookie and a glass of "coconut milk" to wash it down.

She entertained me by singing and dancing to her Hannah Montana CD before leading me around the yard for an "island tour." On our tour around the "island," she renamed every tree, shrub, and flower with a pseudo-Hawaiian name, spoken in her very best Hawaiian accent.

It saddens me to think that she'll grow out of this imaginative play one day and be forced to deal with the pressures of being a teenager as my son has had to do. Knowing that they will have to grow up and face the challenges of adulthood is a stark reality, and my primary objective as their mom is to love them through and prepare them for the changes they will face in the years ahead.

Some days I wish I could simply be a child, but God has called all of us to maturity in him. Life gives us many opportunities to grow in grace and knowledge of our Lord Jesus Christ, and it is our responsibility as Christians and as parents to help those we love do the same. Still, Jesus invites us to come as little children, full of wonder and awe. As you crawl up in his lap today, thank him for the simple pleasures of life and ask him to give you childlike faith to trust in his Word to carry you through each day.

WHO AM I REALLY?

Therefore, if anyone is in Christ, he is a new
creation; the old has gone, the new has come!

2 Corinthians 5:17

Just be yourself. That is a phrase all of us have heard at
one time or another, but who are we really? For the past
several years, God has been at work changing me from
the inside out. I am no longer the person I used to be,
thankfully, but I have yet to become all that God wants
me to be.

God often uses the circumstances of life to chisel away
our character flaws and make us more like him. He places
us in situations that are beyond our control, creating in us
a dependency on him. In our weakness, he shows himself strong (2 Corinthians 12:10). When we lack the basic
necessities of life, he becomes the supplier of all we need
(Philippians 4:19). When we fail to treat one another with

love and respect, he reminds us of his love and mercy for all mankind (John 3:16–17).

We are all works in progress. Every trial and tribulation is meant for our good, not our punishment (James 1:2–4). God supplies the wisdom and all the resources we need to endure the hardships we face in life (James 1:5–6), if we ask him. He gives us his all-surpassing peace to comfort and sustain us in times of trouble (John 14:27; 16:33). When we feel we are alone in our struggles, God encourages and assures us of his abiding presence with us (Deuteronomy 31:8).

When we are at our worst, Christ is at his best. When we question who we really are, we can be certain that God knows us completely (Psalm 139), loves us sacrificially (1 John 4:10), and will be faithful to us even when we are faithless (2 Timothy 2:13).

Who am I really? A beloved child of God, destined for greater things that I can ask or imagine (Ephesians 3:20). So are you.

FORGETTING GOD

The Israelites did what was evil in the LORD's sight; they forgot the LORD their God and worshiped the Baals and the Asherahs.

Judges 3:7

As I read my devotions one morning, I was struck by the truth in the above verse. Written over a thousand years before Christ's birth, these words speak specifically of the Israelites. But could it be said that as twenty-first-century Americans we are also guilty of forgetting God and worshipping our own idols?

So many of society's problems are a direct result of our idolatry. Forgetting God, we have turned to material possessions to fill a void that only God can fill. In our pursuit of happiness, we have filled our lives with things that can never give us the satisfaction that can be had in a personal relationship with Jesus. As a result, we have become enslaved to the very idols we worship, incurring debt we cannot repay and losing any financial freedom we might have.

The same is true of our relationships. Forgetting God, we look for love in places even angels fear to tread, compromising our sexual purity, risking disease and heartbreak, and often winding up alone because we build our life around someone who is ultimately unfaithful and unable to love us as God does.

Forgetting God, we look for satisfaction in our careers, in our children's athletic and academic achievements, and even in our ministries as we get caught up in what we are doing for the Lord. We fail to yield fully to him, allowing him to work through us and to achieve what he desires. We make life about us instead of about him.

The writer of Judges goes on to say, "The Lord's anger burned against Israel, and he sold them to Cushan-rishathaim king of Aram of the Two Rivers, and the Israelites served him eight years" (Judges 3:8). God is a jealous and just God. Is it any wonder that he gives us over to the very idols we worship?

There is hope for us. God has promised to give us all we need if we will give him first place in our lives. Only by surrendering to and worshipping God will we finally break free from the bondage of all that owns us and find true satisfaction and love.

IF I HAD IT TO DO ALL OVER AGAIN

In everything set them an example by doing what is good. In your teaching show integrity, seriousness and soundness of speech that cannot be condemned, so that those who oppose you may be ashamed because they have nothing bad to say about us.

Titus 2:7–8

As we wrapped up our first year of homeschooling, I didn't have to look far to see the mistakes we made or the challenges we had to overcome in order to reach the finish line. Our journey was paved with a variety of experiences—fun field trips; interesting and not-so-interesting lessons; discoveries about our world, human nature, and God's amazing provision; a sense of community with those who helped us find our way; and a level of bonding with my children that I could only have experienced as a homeschooling mom.

As difficult as things were at times, God never abandoned us. Rather he was always beside us to encourage us with his Word and to give me the wisdom I needed to deal with the challenges we faced. Although my children were the students, I think I learned more than both of them combined. God taught me many lessons in patience, understanding, parenting, psychology, and dependence on him. He used the challenges we faced to teach me that there are some things I cannot control and that I must choose my battles and allow my children to learn from their own mistakes. I learned more about my children and myself through this experience than I ever dreamed possible.

We all face challenges that God uses to mold and shape us. The key to growing through our adversities is to allow God to have his way with us in and through the difficulties of daily life. I try not to repeat my mistakes, but sometimes it takes more than one lesson for me to master the concepts God is trying to teach me. God is infinitely patient, though, and never gives up on those of us who desire to truly learn his ways, even though we might on occasion fail the tests he gives us.

What are some of the more difficult challenges you have faced? Even though you might have not have felt God's presence at the time, God was there drawing you near to him. Knowing that in the end you would receive the prize of a more intimate relationship with God, wouldn't you do it all over again?

THIS OR THAT?

Do not be deceived: God cannot be mocked. A man reaps what he sows. The one who sows to please his sinful nature, from that nature will reap destruction; the one who sows to please the Spirit, from the Spirit will reap eternal life.

Galatians 6:7–8

The simple life is a thing of the past. Variety has crept into every aspect of our existence, and we are bombarded with choices. For some, having options is a highly desirable thing; however, many of us long for the simplicity of days gone by.

Going out to dinner as a family can often generate quite a debate as we try to figure out which restaurant to choose. Mexican or Italian? Burgers or pizza? If burgers, which fast-food place? We all have our favorites. Whatever happened to the days of piling into the car and going to the only restaurant in the neighborhood? I find it easier and cheaper these days to simply stock the freezer with convenience foods we can prepare at home.

Some choices carry more weight than deciding what's for dinner, and the consequences of our choices can be far-reaching. The Bible has a lot to say about choices, particularly in the areas of our behaviors and habits, our relationships, and how we spend the resources (time and money) that God entrusts to us.

In the sixth chapter of Galatians, Paul uses an agricultural principle to state a timeless truth: we reap what we sow. This is a concept I try to convey often to my children, especially in the areas of entertainment and social interaction. Experience has taught me that what I allow myself to see, hear, and do really does have lasting consequences. We become desensitized to the violence, profanity, and sensuality that often pervades the programs we watch, and those images and speech patterns are stored in our brain, whether or not we want them to be. If that is the way God designed our minds to work, then why are we so prone to choose entertainment that is less than wholesome?

God has given us the freedom to choose whether to sin or not sin, to love or not love our fellow man, and to live an abundant life in Christ or die in the mediocrity of a worldly existence. It's that simple really. The next time you are faced with choices, I challenge you to go to God's Word and see what he has to say about your options. There is a world of relevant wisdom in the pages of Scripture.

Dee Dee Wike

THE CENTER OF MY UNIVERSE

Do nothing out of selfish ambition or vain conceit, but in humility consider others better than yourselves. Each of you should look not only to your own interests, but also to the interests of others. Your attitude should be the same as that of Christ Jesus.

Philippians 2:3–5

Everything we do in life—every decision we make—can directly impact not only ourselves but others as well. Yet often we don't stop to consider the consequences our poor choices may have on other people. This is a truth I see played out in my own family day in and day out. We make so much of life about ourselves, as though we are the center of our own universe.

If I was to take an honest look at myself and all the decisions I make, I would have to answer the basic question, "Who am I living for?" When I make the choice to use a credit card in order to purchase something non-essential, am I doing that to satisfy a desire I have, or do I have my family's best interests in mind? Years of frivolous spending have taught me that although I think I might be doing the right thing at the time, I am actually doing harm to my family by making a bad financial position even worse. Momentary pleasure can reap long-term consequences in some very unpleasant ways.

Even when I consider my problems, some of which were brought on by circumstances beyond my control, do I ask, "Why me?" or do I ask, "Why not me?" Do my attitudes and actions under pressure reflect the belief that God is in control or that I am?

I believe one reason we live such defeated lives is that too often we turn our gaze inward, focusing on our own problems, rather than outward, where we can look into the lives of others. We get caught up in our own dilemma, seldom considering that others are going through difficulties far worse than our own or refusing to believe that anyone could understand how heavy our burden is. There is one who understands. His name is Jesus.

Everything Jesus did was motivated by his love for humanity. He came to serve, not to be served. He came to love those who were unlovable, to forgive those who had done the unforgivable, and to free those in bondage to their own sinful desires. He could have saved himself from crucifixion, but he chose to lay down his life in order that we might live forever.

Christ did not live for himself; he lived for you and me. Jesus wants to be the center of your universe, the light that shines in your darkness, and the source of your peace. You won't find peace by looking inward. You will only find his love, peace, and provision as you turn your gaze away from yourself and fix your eyes on him.

ONE WORD

May my cry come before you, O LORD; give me understanding according to your word. May my supplication come before you; deliver me according to your promise.

Psalm 119:169–170

My One Word (www.myoneword.org) is an experiment designed to encourage us to think about our lives, toss the long list of changes we would like to make, and pick one word that describes our character and the vision we have for our lives. When I think about this, it is difficult for me to pick just one word (an occupational hazard for a writer, I suppose), yet God often does that with me during my quiet time with him each day. For example, the theme of all three devotionals I read one morning was "wait," as in wait on God's direction, answers to prayer, and on his revelation of truth to me.

Dee Dee Wike

I believe that quite often we get so caught up in the mechanics of having a quiet time, we make it more of a chore than it should be, and we become frustrated. Somehow it becomes easier to just go on with our day rather than try to figure out what God is trying to tell us in his Word. Or perhaps we don't consider his Word adequate to do the job of imparting the wisdom and direction we need to deal with our circumstances so we start seeking answers from other sources, which becomes not only confusing but also dangerous.

The next time you sit down with your Bible and a favorite devotional, before you begin reading ask the Holy Spirit to impress upon you just one word of truth. Read Scripture in the context in which it was written, without reading anything into it. Learn to take God at his Word and know that you can confidently stand on the promises of Scripture. You don't need philosophers, self-help gurus, or talk show hosts to help you figure out life. You just need one word—God's Word.

HOLDING
ONTO HOPE

And we rejoice in the hope of the glory of God.
Not only so, but we also rejoice in our sufferings,
because we know that suffering produces
perseverance; perseverance, character; and
character, hope. And hope does not disappoint
us, because God has poured out his love into our
hearts by the Holy Spirit, whom he has given us.

Romans 5:2b–5

Every day, I am grateful for the richness of God's blessings, his love, his provision, and his peace in my life. But
I know some who are suffering the cruel shock of a loved
one's unexpected death, the loss of a job, and the heartache that accompanies addiction and broken relationships. They are reeling from the suffering that God has

allowed in their lives. What is the purpose in their pain, and how can they get through the difficulties they face? Is there hope that things will get better?

As I ponder these questions and God's sovereignty in allowing bad things to happen to good people, I instinctively turn to the Bible for answers. God's Word is my lifeline when the storms of life overwhelm me. Because we are human, our understanding of his ways is limited (Isaiah 55:9). Often we cannot see God's purpose in our pain, but we are told in Scripture that he cares for us (1 Peter 5:7), he has a purpose and plan for our lives (Jeremiah 29:11), and he uses our adversity to build godly character in us (Romans 5:4) and bring glory to himself (John 11:4). Knowing his Word gives us the assurance that he is with us and will not forsake us (Deuteronomy 31:8), that he knows where we are (Job 23:10), and that he loves us and will provide everything we need, including his grace, to make it through, one day at a time (Matthew 6:33; 2 Corinthians 9:8).

All of these assurances are fine for me, but what about those who are struggling? The beauty of God's promises is that they are written for *all* who believe, whether we are in seasons of lack or gain, joy or sorrow, sickness or health. "Every word of God is flawless; he is a shield to those who take refuge in him" (Proverbs 30:5). If we are to have hope, we must believe God's Word to be true and take refuge in him.

THE PERFECT GIFT

Thanks be to God for his indescribable gift!
2 Corinthians 9:15

It seems strange to think of it now, but I remember well the very first Christmas present my sweet husband gave me. We started dating in November 1985, just after my birthday, and spent much of our time together at a local health club. Somehow, Steve thought that ankle weights might make the perfect gift for our first Christmas together. Ankle weights! Can you even imagine?

I have to think that my husband was a little nervous about that first Christmas together, or perhaps so blinded by love that he would come up with such an unusual gift for me. Little did he know how quickly I exchanged those ankle weights for something I might actually wear. Bless his heart! He must have known how eager I was to shed

Dee Dee Wike

a few pounds and thought the gift might help speed up the process.

Some girls might not even give a guy a second chance after receiving a gift like that, but I knew from the start that Steve was God's special gift to me. Nearly twenty-five years of marriage have proved my judgment on that matter to be flawless. I am pleased to say that Steve now excels in his gift giving, even when money is tight, and that I love not only his gifts but the giver himself.

God knows all about giving gifts to his children. He provides everything we need for daily life and occasionally throws in an extra blessing just because he loves us. His ultimate gift to us—his perfect gift—is Jesus Christ, his only Son. Wrapped in the Father's love, he came to live among us, as one of us, and made it possible for us to spend eternity with God by giving up his very life on the cross. He died for our sins that we might become righteous and worthy of living with him in heaven for all eternity.

Salvation is Christ's free gift to us. His grace is ours to receive if we but choose to acknowledge our sin and ask his forgiveness. Will you accept his perfect gift today?

MADE FOR MINISTRY

For we are God's workmanship, created in Christ Jesus to do good works, which God prepared in advance for us to do.

Ephesians 2:10

As I was out walking one morning and praying about the lessons God has taught me, the places he has taken me, and the doors I pray he will open before me, the thought occurred to me that we are all made for ministry. There is something of great significance that he has called each of us to do, whether or not there is great visibility or extrinsic rewards for our calling. A stay-at-home mom or corporate executive is no less a minister than an ordained pastor. Our pulpit is just different. Some of us minister to our own families and coworkers, but our message is the same: "For God so loved the world that he gave his one and only Son, that whoever believes in him shall not perish but have eternal life" (John 3:16).

Everything we do in life should point others to the cross of Christ and glorify our Father who is in heaven. Our speech, countenance, and attitude should reflect the love and grace of God. Our service should be directed toward others rather than ourselves. The unique gifts God has given each of us should be used for his glory to reach the lost and encourage those who walk beside us every day.

Where has God placed you today? Whether you are in the spotlight or cleaning out the closet, know that you were uniquely made for the ministry to which God has appointed you. Rejoice that you are part of something much bigger than your eyes can see and that nothing you do goes unnoticed by God. Others may not see your good works, but God does, and his smile lights up the heavens when you serve him with all your heart.

PUTREFIED
OR PURIFIED?

We all stumble in many ways. If anyone is never at fault in what he says, he is a perfect man, able to keep his whole body in check.

James 3:2

As I was meandering on one of the social networks this morning, I ran across a variety of comments from a veritable cross-section of the population. Some of the things I read were encouraging and uplifting; others saddened me greatly. When is the last time any of us stopped to consider how God would feel reading our comments? Would he consider our words putrefied as a result of our sinful nature or find them to be a reflection of a heart that has

Dee Dee Wike

been purified? What about others who know us? Would they be shocked by some of the comments we post?

All too often we speak before we think, hastily expressing ourselves in ways that are inconsistent with the character of Christ. We are quick to become angry and to speak harshly and slow to listen to those around us. The Bible says we are to do just the opposite: "Everyone should be quick to listen, slow to speak and slow to become angry, for man's anger does not bring about the righteous life that God desires" (James 1:19–20). I am dreadfully guilty of this. Are you?

God desires for our speech to be pure, for our lives to be a reflection of his holiness (1 Peter 1:16), and for all of us "to set an example for the believers in speech, in life, in love, in faith, and in purity" (1 Timothy 4:12). God will never wash our mouths out with soap, but he desires to make us holy, cleansing us "by the washing with water through the word so that he can present us to himself as a radiant church, without stain or wrinkle or any other blemish, but holy and blameless" (Ephesians 5:26–27).

If your speech and actions don't reflect the character of Christ, take a few moments to confess your sin and seek his forgiveness. He loves you no matter what you say or do. He wants to use you to reach the lost and encourage those around you. "Do not let any unwholesome talk come out of your mouths, but only what is helpful for building others up according to their needs, that it may benefit those who listen" (Ephesians 4:29). Instead, "let your conversation be always full of grace, seasoned with salt, so that you may know how to answer everyone" (Colossians 4:6).

ONCE
UPON A TIME

But these things are written that you may believe
that Jesus is the Christ, the Son of God, and that
by believing you may have life in his name.

John 20:31

Each of us has a story to tell, and every day we are writing our own story whether we realize it or not. Each day in our lives becomes a paragraph; each season, a chapter. What we allow people to see becomes the book cover. What does your book say about you?

No matter whether your story is expressed verbally, through your actions, or in writing, your life communicates a message to those around you. Is yours a message of hope and encouragement or one of misery and futility? If

God opened your book and read what you have written, would he see himself as the main character and hero of your book?

God has written the most popular book of all time, the Bible, through the inspiration of his Holy Spirit. From cover to cover, he has included you in it. Have you taken the time to read his love letter to you or taken hold of the promises he has made to you? If not, what are you waiting for?

So often we read books for entertainment or self-improvement, but the Bible is so much more. Filled with mystery, romance, adventure, and practical help, it is a book that will revolutionize the way you live your life, and more importantly, help you know the God who created you, the Savior who redeemed you, and the Spirit who empowers you to face victoriously the challenges of each day. If you don't own a copy, buy or borrow one. If you have a Bible and don't read it, you are missing out on the greatest story ever told.

God is crazy about you. Don't take my word for it; take his. It's right there in the pages of your Bible.

NOTHING NEW UNDER THE SUN

> Fear God and keep his commandments, for this is
> the whole duty of man. For God will bring every
> deed into judgment, including every hidden thing,
> whether it is good or evil.
>
> Ecclesiastes 12:13–14

The sun often shines where I live, but sometimes a cloud of reality hovers over me: "What has been will be again, what has been done will be done again; there is nothing new under the sun" (Ecclesiastes 1:9).

Life is but a series of unending cycles. We are born, we live, and we die. We see this in nature as cold and dreary winter strips the earth of living, colorful vegetation, and spring heralds the return of life in all its glory. We also see

Dee Dee Wike

it in the responsibilities of daily life. Although we labor diligently to earn a paycheck, the money goes as quickly as it comes. Every chore we complete has to be repeated over and over again. We make progress, but there is always something more to be done.

The same can be said of our spiritual lives. Some of us look for God in the details of our lives, deliberately seeking a deeper relationship with him through prayer, Bible study, and fellowship with other Christians. Others of us run from him or at least put him on a shelf, convinced that we are able to live life on our own terms. We walk through our days with hardly a thought of God, never knowing the joy, peace, and sense of purpose we forfeit because we exclude him from the very lives he created us to live.

Many years ago, I learned the hard way that the grass is not always greener on the other side. Living life on my own terms brought only misery, heartache, and trouble for me in the form of addictions, bad relationships, and poor financial habits. Sure, I was successful in my career, had nice things, and traveled to some pretty nice places, but none of it filled the empty void created for God to fill. Although a lifelong believer in God and the commandments in his Word, I often chose to disobey and disregard them. True to his Word, God held me accountable for and allowed me to suffer the consequences of my sinful choices.

God is just, and he will judge each of us when we stand before him. But God is also loving and merciful. He is ready to receive any child of his who is truly repentant and ready to turn from his sin.

Certainly, we may get tired of the same old headlines, the repetitious chores and responsibilities, and the never-ending ups and downs of life, but we can know that this world is not all there is. We have a home waiting for us in heaven, and one day we will be in the presence of the one who waits for us there. While we are still in this world, we must continue to live each day according to his Word, share the love of God with those around us, and strive to make a positive difference in the lives of others for his glory.

A HEALTHY OBSESSION

I have been crucified with Christ and I no longer live, but Christ lives in me. The life I live in the body, I live by faith in the Son of God, who loved me and gave himself for me.

Galatians 2:20

We live in a culture that caters to and encourages obsession. From the commercials we see on television and the sale ads that appear in our Sunday newspaper, it is clear that corporate America is fostering obsession—often unhealthy obsession—with everything from the clothes we wear and the cars we drive to the way we treat our bodies in order to attain an image of perfection.

Beyond the obvious, however, there are other obsessions to consider that might not seem so apparent. Because of our current economy many of us are obsessed with worry over our personal finances. We are so fearful that we might lose everything we have that we become tightfisted and reluctant to reach out to those in need. We are bombarded with negative headlines daily that cause us to fear the worst for our families. The more we are immersed in the pessimism that is rampant in our society, the more prone we are to buy into the hopelessness that anything will change for the better.

Oswald Chambers, in *My Utmost for His Highest*, writes:

> If we are obsessed by God, nothing else can get into our lives – not concerns, nor tribulation, nor worries. How dare we to be so absolutely unbelieving when God totally surrounds us? To be obsessed by God is to have an effective barricade against all the assaults of the enemy.[2]

What is your obsession today? Is it the fear of financial ruin, the ongoing struggle with a wayward child, or the uncertainty of the future? Living in this world will never be easy, but if we will live as those who have been crucified with Christ, allowing him to live in us, then we will find the strength and courage to face whatever comes our way.

THE CLOCK
IS TICKING

Satisfy us in the morning with your unfailing love,
that we may sing for joy and be glad all our days.
Make us glad for as many days as you have afflicted
us, for as many years as we have seen trouble.

Psalm 90:14–15

I am obsessed with time management and am often frustrated by people, especially those in my household, who do not make good use of their time. In my mind, time is a gift from God that should be used wisely, not squandered. Keenly aware that the clock is ticking and that time is running out for completing the school year, preparing my children for adulthood and doing any of a number of other things that are time-sensitive, I find myself wound a little too tightly some days. When my driven personality begins to drive me (and everyone around me) crazy, then it becomes necessary for me to take some time off!

God is the creator and keeper of time. He holds eternity in his hands and has placed it in our hearts. We live in a world that is coming to an end with a sense of urgency that we must do all we can to bring him glory and to reach the lost who don't know him. Yet God desires that we take the time daily to enjoy life and especially to enjoy an intimate relationship with him. If we don't stop long enough to acknowledge him, read his Word, and talk with him in prayer, how can we truly enjoy anything? God is the giver of all our blessings, yet often we fail to even thank him.

Today, take the day off to enjoy your family, the beauty of God's creation, and most of all, God himself. As a wise individual once told me, "Do what you can and don't worry about the rest. It will be there tomorrow." God created us as human beings, not "human doings," so put the to-do list on hold, relax, and rejoice in the Lord!

SUMMERTIME, AND THE LIVIN' IS...

He will not let your foot slip—he who watches
over you will not slumber; indeed, he who watches
over Israel will neither slumber nor sleep.

Psalm 121:3–4

"Summertime" is perhaps the best-known song from
George Gershwin's American folk opera, Porgy and
Bess. While summertime brings easy living for many as
the school year ends and the lazy, hazy days of summer
replace the normal routines of everyday life, some of us
remain as busy as ever. The grass and weeds in my yard
don't take a vacation; neither do the laundry and house-
work inside. My husband continues to work through the
summer months so we can pay the bills, while I manage

the household, shop for curriculum, and make plans for the next school year.

Still, I love summer because it gives us options we don't have at other times of the year. The pool at the YMCA is always a welcome diversion, and the coming and going of my kids and their friends is an indescribable pleasure. Occasionally, their activities take them away from the house, resulting in periods of peaceful solitude when I can think and write and work on some of my projects.

Many of us view summer vacation as a needed break from our daily routines and responsibilities and a chance to reconnect with our families. We are eager to plan and pack for our getaways, excited about seeing new places and experiencing new things. However, as our vacation winds down and reality inevitably sets in, we begin to wonder if a brief vacation was really worth the monetary cost or the extra work awaiting us at work and at home.

Life never takes a vacation; fortunately, neither does God. No matter where we are, whether at Disneyworld or digging ourselves out of another stressful situation, he is there. Sometimes I wonder if God ever wants to go on vacation and get away from his routine of always providing, always guiding, and always answering the prayers of his children. He neither slumbers nor sleeps (Psalm 121:4), yet somehow he never burns out as the rest of us do.

As you make plans for your summer vacation or "stay-cation," remember that God is with you. Resolve to slow down a little, even if your routine doesn't, and look for little ways to vacation each day. One of my favorite ways to do that is to grab an ice-cream cone with my kids and walk through the town square or the nature center at our local park. If we make a deliberate effort to set aside a few minutes each day to relax and enjoy the simple pleasures of life and the people we love, we will find ourselves refreshed, restored, and renewed.

HEARING VOICES

Be still, and know that I am God; I will be exalted
among the nations, I will be exalted in the earth.
Psalm 46:10

Recently when I took my dog for her bedtime walk, I
did what she often does. I just stood there and listened
to the sounds of the world around me. Madison irritates
me at times, taking longer than necessary for her routine
because she is so wrapped up in the sounds and smells of
her surroundings. As I stood there taking in the refreshing breeze of an unseasonably cool summer evening, I listened to the sound of the wind in the treetops, hoping to
hear a whisper from the Lord.

The problem with most of us is that we are so busy
pursuing our own agendas that we don't stop long enough
to listen for God's still, small voice or to even acknowledge that he exists. We run around conducting our usual

affairs, listening to the voice of reason or talk show hosts whose message of hope and inspiration couldn't be further from the truth of God's Word. How much better might our lives be if we actually took the time to listen to and follow the voice of our Lord Jesus?

In John 10, Jesus calls himself our shepherd and warns us of the thief who comes only to steal and kill and destroy (v. 10). He says,

> He (the Shepherd) calls his own sheep by name and leads them out. When he has brought out all his own, he goes on ahead of them, and his sheep follow him because they know his voice. But they will never follow a stranger; in fact, they will run away from him because they do not recognize a stranger's voice.
>
> John 10:3–5

Whose voice will you listen to today? Will you heed the voice of the good shepherd, who loves you and will guide you in the way of truth, or will you be led astray by the voice of the enemy who seeks only to steal, kill, and destroy? Take a few moments each day to seek out the shepherd in prayer, to learn truth from his Word, and to become familiar with the sound of his voice. When you begin to walk with him, you will fall in love with him and realize that he is all you need.

NOT MY OWN

May the words of my mouth and the meditation
of my heart be pleasing in your sight, O LORD, my
Rock and my Redeemer.

Psalm 19:14

As I was reading through a familiar passage of Scripture
one morning, I came across words I had never quite seen
before. When I substituted the word *write* for the word
say, the verse took on new meaning for me. "The words
I say (write) to you are not just my own. Rather, it is the
Father, living in me, who is doing his work" (John 14:10b).

The words I write each day truly are not just my own.
As I blog about the circumstances and challenges of life, it
is with the purpose of applying God's Word to the issues
we all face and to draw wisdom from the Scriptures. My
prayer is that my readers see that God's Word truly is relevant and that God cares about the details of our lives. I

Dee Dee Wike

write not to be heard, but to show others that God is present in the ordinary and extraordinary events that happen all around us.

God desires to be the center of our lives. From the moment we awake in the morning to the minute we close our eyes in peaceful slumber, he wants us to grow deeper in our knowledge of his Word and in our relationship with him. He is a personal God who wants to share in every aspect of our lives, and he longs for fellowship with his created ones. Because of his great love and mercy, he is willing to forgive any sin that stands between us and him.

Do you know Jesus? Take it from one who once wandered far from the fold—there is no sin in your life that Jesus can't forgive, no hurt he can't heal, no problem he can't solve. But Jesus will not impose himself on you. He is standing just outside your door, waiting for you to invite him in.

HORSING AROUND

He who fears the LORD has a secure fortress, and
for his children it will be a refuge. The fear of the
LORD is a fountain of life, turning a man from the
snares of death.

Proverbs 14:26–27

One summer evening, my daughter and I attended a char-
ity horse show. Because of Joy's budding interest in horses, I
thought it might be nice to take her to a horse show where
she could enjoy the beauty and athleticism of the sport.

Since Joy had expressed an interest in riding lessons,
I began looking into lessons and summer horse camps to
foster a love of, rather than a fear of, these splendid animals. After riding a runaway horse as a teenager, I swore
that if I lived to get off that horse, I would never go near
another one.

Dee Dee Wike

Long before Joy attended horse camp, I contacted my friend, Ann, who has raised and shown quarter horses for a long time. We visited her stable, and she immediately put Joy to work brushing, bridling, and saddling her show horse. She helped Joy lead the horse into the corral, taught Joy a few simple handling commands, and walked the horse around the ring while Joy sat high and proud in the saddle. It was a thrill for both Joy and me to be that close to such a splendid animal. We both learned a lot about horses, and I found my fear of them greatly diminished.

Fear is nothing to horse around with. While it can often keep us out of dangerous situations, it can also keep us from enjoying experiences that enrich our lives. During our trip to Ann's stable, I learned that knowledge can dispel fear and increase our appreciation of the very thing that caused us fear in the first place.

The Bible tells us, "The fear of the LORD is the beginning of knowledge, but fools despise wisdom and discipline" (Proverbs 1:7) and "the fear of the LORD teaches a man wisdom, and humility comes before honor" (Proverbs 15:33). The fear of the LORD is not fear as we know it, the state of being fearful, but rather an awe and reverence for God. As we fear God and come to know him, and as we study his Word, we become less fearful of the world around us. God promises us his protection, his provision, and his peace in the midst of our difficult circumstances.

What are you afraid of today? Financial ruin, devastating illness, emotional pain? Search God's Word for truth and wisdom regarding that which causes you fear. Seek a deeper knowledge of God himself and rest in the promises of his Word.

"When I am afraid, I will trust in you. In God, whose word I praise, in God I trust; I will not be afraid. What can mortal man do to me?" (Psalm 56:3–4).

God loves you perfectly, and his love casts out fear (1 John 4:18).

I DO BELIEVE
IN ANGELS

For he will command his angels concerning you to
guard you in all your ways.

Psalm 91:11

While vacationing in Florida, God protected us from
an angry driver after a late-night collision. His car came
out of nowhere, hit us, and we witnessed his rage turn to
remorse. Although his car was badly damaged, ours had
only one little nick in the fender. No police were called,
we sustained no bodily injuries—the whole incident was
but a blip on the radar of our lives.

Just a few months later, our family was driving through
midtown Memphis in search of a restaurant. As we
approached a busy intersection driving in the middle lane,

a speeding motorcycle zoomed past on the right side and cut in front of our car, missing our bumper only because I immediately slowed down to give him room when I caught him out of the corner of my eye. Not realizing it until a police car sped past us on the left side with lights and sirens going, we found ourselves in the middle of a high-speed chase.

As the police car proceeded through the intersection, the driver of the squad car suddenly hit his brakes, went into a spin, and collided with a car just a few yards in front of us. As car parts flew off both vehicles and the damaged police cruiser skidded through the intersection and came to an abrupt stop, not only were we amazed by what we had just witnessed, but we were also overwhelmed by the realization that God's angels were surrounding and protecting us.

I realize that having a paperclip angel and handmade cross hanging from my rearview mirror have absolutely nothing to do with the fact that we emerged from both accidents unscathed. However, it does serve as a daily reminder and encouragement that God does send his angels to protect my family when we are running errands, enjoying a family night out, or traveling to a vacation destination. God sends his angels with my children every time they leave home to play or hang out with friends. If I didn't have that assurance, I would never let my children go anywhere.

Who is watching over you today? Have you surrendered your heart and entrusted your life to Jesus, or will you dare to go through another day in your own strength and power? I have lived enough days taking care of myself and my affairs to know that God does it much better than I ever could. Trust him today to take care of all that concerns you.

ALL ABOUT ARITHMETIC

Give, and it will be given to you. A good measure, pressed down, shaken together and running over, will be poured into your lap. For with the measure you use, it will be measured to you.

Luke 6:38

In the summer of 2009, we were all about arithmetic. I was teaching my son algebra in preparation for his sophomore year and was re-learning the concepts I learned more years ago than I can count. The older I get, the more I appreciate mathematics. Hopefully, my son will eventually learn to appreciate math as well.

God is all about math too. He created math and the concepts of addition, subtraction, multiplication, and divi-

Dee Dee Wike

sion. One doesn't have to look far in God's Word to see the many ways God has used math since the beginning of time. From the pairing of animals brought onto the ark to the precise measurements of the ark Noah built to protect them from the flood, God used numbers. Interestingly, though, he created only one you. Of all the billions of people who have lived, currently live, or will live on this planet, no one else is like you.

God's math seems illogical to us. We tend to hold onto the money and possessions we own because we are afraid of losing what we have. God, however, commands us to give and lend freely to others, even if it means we must sacrifice in order to obey him. In God's economy, giving to others does not diminish our treasure but rather increases it. When we give to those in need, God provides for our needs and gives us joy in return. Jesus himself said, "It is more blessed to give than to receive" (Acts 20:35).

Are you in need today? Whether your need is monetary or you simply lack encouragement, look beyond your need to see how you can help meet someone else's needs. Do the math. God is counting on you to give to others so they, in turn, may receive the greatest treasure of all—salvation in Jesus Christ.

FINDING FAVOR
WITH GOD

May the favor of the Lord our God rest upon us; establish the work of our hands for us—yes, establish the work of our hands.

Psalm 90:17

Living on one income and determined to reduce our monthly expenses, I contacted our phone service provider to find ways to reduce the monthly charges for our landline, cell phone, and Internet service. Although it was a time-consuming process, I was successful in accomplishing my objective of saving money, thanks to God's favor and some very helpful customer service representatives.

I have found that God's favor can come in any size. For some, it may come as an inheritance, a substantial bonus, or a job promotion. For most of us, however, his favor comes in small packages every day, such as green lights in traffic when we're running late for an appointment. God's favor is not limited to our financial matters. The key to experiencing his favor in every area of life is to have a grateful and expectant heart, know and obey his Word, and surrender every aspect of our lives to him.

God desires to give good gifts to his children (Matthew 7:11), but he requires us to be faithful with what he entrusts to us. God is not in the bailout business, and it is not likely that he will send me a big check in the mail. I believe the favor I have received in my dealings with the phone company are a direct result of my efforts to correct some bad financial habits and be a better steward of all that God has given my family. My financial troubles are largely the result of unwise decisions in the past, but God demonstrates his grace and favor daily as he provides for the needs of our family.

I truly believe that as we continue to correct bad habits, commit to God all he has given to us, and handle our finances according to scriptural principles, he will bless us in some unexpected ways. "Let us not become weary in doing good, for at the proper time we will reap a harvest if we do not give up. Therefore, as we have opportunity, let us do good to all people, especially to those who belong to the family of believers" (Galatians 6:9–10).

MY GREAT REWARD

He regarded disgrace for the sake of Christ as of greater value than the treasures of Egypt, because he was looking ahead to his reward.

Hebrews 11:26

As our pastor read Hebrews 11:26 during our Bible study last night, I was struck by the phrase, "Because he was looking ahead to his reward." We had been talking about the great biblical heroes of faith and their challenges and triumphs. What faith they had, and what great faith we need. It seems that the struggles of our lives intensify with each passing day. But no matter how difficult life can be, we have the assurance that God is with us, that this life is not all there is, and that our reward in heaven will be great (Luke 6:23).

We don't have to wait until we get to heaven to claim our reward, however. God himself is our reward (Genesis

Dee Dee Wike

15:1). When we are discouraged and weary from the battle, his Word is our encouragement. We can know that his promises are true and that we can count on him to see us through every struggle, pain, and heartache. When we face our trials with perseverance and allow perseverance to finish its work, we will be mature and complete, not lacking anything (James 1:4). God is with us always, even in the most difficult circumstances. He is always teaching us something new, even in the heat of adversity. When he has tested us, we shall come forth as gold (Job 23:10).

God is with you and will be faithful to see you through your most difficult challenges. Look for him, lean on him, and know that as you earnestly seek and place your faith in him, he will reward you (Hebrews 11:6).

IT'S FOR YOUR OWN GOOD

No discipline seems pleasant at the time, but painful. Later on, however, it produces a harvest of righteousness and peace for those who have been trained by it.

Hebrews 12:11

Even though it was summer, my kids and I continued to homeschool, not by choice, but of necessity. Due to unforeseen circumstances during our first year of home-school, we fell short in a couple of areas and had to do some extra work in algebra, history, and English in order to be ready for the coming school year. None of us was happy about having to do summer school; nonetheless, we worked our way through it and tried to find pockets of pleasure along the way.

One of the lessons I want to instill in my children while they are still in school is the need for discipline in the area of academics. More than learning math or grammar, I want them to learn good study habits and develop a strong work ethic. These are skills they will be able to use in every aspect of their lives, not simply in school.

The process is painstaking at times, both for them and me. We are learning that discipline, while seldom pleasant, is always for our good. "Our fathers disciplined us for a little while as they thought best; but God disciplines us for our good, that we may share in his holiness" (Hebrews 12:10). God is a loving father who cares deeply for his children. Sometimes his discipline seems harsh and unnecessary to us, but when we yield to it, he always brings a good result in the end. Oh, how I want my children to realize that my motivation in disciplining them is the same—to see them grow in grace, knowledge, righteousness, and peace.

Even as "the Lord disciplines those He loves, as a father the son he delights in" (Proverbs 3:12), I want my children to know that my discipline is motivated out of love and concern for their present and future well-being. I want them to learn that as we all submit ourselves to the discipline of our loving heavenly Father, we will reap the righteousness and peace that he has promised us.

THE END
OF AN ERA

The heavens declare the glory of God; the skies proclaim the work of his hands. Day after day they pour forth speech; night after night they display knowledge. There is no speech or language where their voice is not heard.

Psalm 19:1–2

On June 13, 2009, I witnessed history in the making as I watched my favorite television station flip the switch at 9:23 a.m., effectively eradicating analog television and killing the signal to two of our TV sets. Many people lost their TV signals and one of their primary connections with the outside world. Although our family purchased a digital converter months ago, we found ourselves wishing for the old analog signal as the weather turned

Dee Dee Wike

severe. How interesting that the weather would turn so bad the very day that the entire country went to digital broadcasting.

Because of intense lightning, I unplugged the only set in my house connected to a digital converter and frantically searched for a radio station that carried weather coverage. As it turned out, we were spared the brunt of the storm, but I felt so lost without my TV. It is scary to think that we have become so dependent on technology that we don't function well without it. I am thankful the weather service has the technology to forecast and warn us about severe weather, but I often wish that my own life wasn't quite so technology-driven. As I write this, my cell phone is charging, our family is watching TV, and my son is waiting for his chance to communicate with his friends on Facebook.

God doesn't need technology to communicate with his children. He has the stars, the moon, the storms, and the sunsets and rainbows that often follow them. Have you seen him today?

PARENTHOOD IS NOT CHILD'S PLAY

These commandments that I give you today are to be upon your hearts. Impress them on your children. Talk about them when you sit at home and when you walk along the road, when you lie down and when you get up.

Deuteronomy 6:6–7

One of my favorite childhood games was "Mother, May I?" Do you remember it? There would be a "mother" at one end of the room, and each of the kids at the other end would take turns asking, "Mother, may I?" The designated mother would say, "Yes, you may…" or "No, you must…" No matter what action I was told to take, my hope was always that I would be the first to reach "mother" and win the game.

Dee Dee Wike

These days, when my kids ask, "Mother, may I?" my answer is often a little more complicated than a simple yes or no. If my teenager wants to stay out with friends, there are always questions I feel compelled to ask him before giving him permission. "Whom are you going with? Where are you going? Is it okay with his or her parents? Will a grownup be there?" There is also the negotiation of a curfew and the appropriate parental admonition to "remember whose you are." How I wish that parenting could be as simple as playing a game of "Mother, May I?" Although my parents certainly had their challenges when I was growing up, society has changed so much that parenting has become a very complicated and exhausting responsibility.

One thing that hasn't changed about parenting is the tremendous amount of love and attention our children need in order to become healthy, well-adjusted adults. Yet many of us spend less time with our children than ever. We have allowed technology to step in and become their babysitter, their primary source of entertainment, and a substitute for the time we could, but often don't spend with them.

Rather than take the time to teach them godly values, we allow the ungodly values of our society to creep into their lives through the TV programs and movies we let them watch, the music they listen to, and the books they read. We don't really monitor, or even discuss, the spiritual and moral implications of their choices. Instead, we leave much to their immature judgment, or worse, simply turn and look the other way, hoping that the consequences of their choices won't be too bad and everything will work itself out in the end.

Just as a pastor shepherds his congregation and ministers to the needs of his flock, so must we guide our children to live according to God's Word and provide the loving, nurturing care that Jesus provided his spiritual children. We cannot leave parenting to chance or fight the good fight only when we have the physical, mental, and emotional strength to do so. We must be vigilant to pray for God's strength, wisdom, grace, and guidance and raise our children with much love and understanding, even and especially when our desire is to do just the opposite. Our kids are facing giants we never knew existed when we were their age. They need the boundaries and affection that only parents can establish and demonstrate. They need heroes who will stand in the gap, help them fight their battles, and wisely discern when it is time to let them find their wings.

As one who gave up a fulfilling position in full-time Christian ministry in order to return to the mission field as a stay-at-home mom, I can say with all conviction that parenting is, at least for me, a far greater calling than any other job I have held. As parents, we are raising the next generation of believers. Look around you—we can't afford to neglect this God-given responsibility. If we don't pour everything we have into our children, and "walk the walk" of authentic Christianity before them, then what hope do they have of discovering and walking in true spiritual freedom and leaving behind a legacy of faith in a society that has become hostile toward Christians?

As parents, God is calling us to wake up, stand up, and unashamedly speak truth to our generation and to our children's generation. Our children need heroes. God needs warriors. Take up the shield of faith, stand firm on the promises of God's Word, and assume your place in his army. The enemy is fierce, and the stakes are high, but the battle belongs to the Lord. Take heart and fight with all that is within you—the victory has been won.

CALLED TO PEACE

Let the peace of Christ rule in your hearts, since
as members of one body you were called to peace.
Colossians 3:15

My quiet time varies from day to day, but one thing I read
with consistency is the devotional from *Our Daily Bread*.
In a recent selection, the Scripture reading was Colossians
3:14–25. Although the author used the verses to write a
devotional on fatherhood, the Lord showed me something entirely different in the verses I read.

Not only does Paul address the body of Christ, the
church, but he also addresses family life issues in these
verses. Whether in our own families or in our church
family, we all have challenging relationships, which
often cause us to experience anything but peace. Yet he
tells us that we are "called to peace." What is this peace?
According to the footnote in my NIV Study Bible, it is "the

Dee Dee Wike

attitude of peace that Christ alone gives—in place of the attitude of bitterness and quarrelsomeness. This attitude is to 'rule' (literally 'function like an umpire') in all human relationships."

What a word this is for me and for all those like me who struggle with challenging relationships. God has called us to peace, to let the peace of Christ rule in our hearts, yet so often we do just the opposite.

How do we achieve or attain this attitude of peace that Christ alone gives? Isaiah 26:3 says, "You will keep in perfect peace him whose mind is steadfast, because he trusts in you." What is steadfastness? It is the state of being firm, fixed, and faithful in our devotion and trust in God, no matter what the circumstances.

What is your mind fixed on today? Is it on your problems and the difficult people in your life, or is your mind fixed on God, whose peace transcends all understanding (Philippians 4:7)? "For he himself is our peace, who has made the two one and has destroyed the barrier, the dividing wall of hostility" (Ephesians 2:14).

AN ERUPTION DISRUPTION

A fool gives full vent to his anger, but a wise man keeps himself under control.

Proverbs 29:11

A couple of my friends traveled to England to visit relatives and found themselves in quite a predicament. The untimely eruption of an Icelandic volcano disrupted air travel for several days, stranding them and delaying their travel well beyond their scheduled return date. Apparently, this volcanic eruption caused more trouble than anyone bargained for, effectively causing European air travel to come to a grinding halt, adversely affecting the economies of the countries involved and seriously inconveniencing countless people who found themselves stuck in airports all across the continent.

Volcanoes are not the only things that can erupt and cause serious damage. Quite often we ourselves can seethe with anger and let things boil beneath the surface until—*wham!* We blow our tops, spewing words that have the potential of causing serious harm. When we find ourselves stewing over things and people that frustrate us, how can we avoid a catastrophic encounter that will leave us or our loved ones feeling burned by the hot lava of hateful words spoken in the heat of the moment? How can we keep from letting our anger get so out of hand that it reaches the boiling point in the first place? This is a problem I struggle with, even on good days, and one I know I cannot conquer without God's divine intervention.

While there is little any of us can do to control a volcano, we can, with God's help, control our own volatile emotions. To do this, we must immerse ourselves in the Word of God so that we know how God would have us act and react toward those people who have a tendency to hurt or anger us. God's Word is richer with wisdom than volcanic soil is with nutrients. As we take in the nourishing truth of God's Word, he strengthens us and causes us to grow, enabling us to deal with our emotions in a healthy and constructive way rather than a harmful and destructive way.

As we read his Word, God reveals areas of sin in our own lives. By confessing those sins and receiving his forgiveness, we make room for his Holy Spirit to live in and through us, supernaturally enabling us to walk in his mercy, love, and grace rather than in bondage to our own flawed humanity.

TO BOLDLY GO
WHERE NO MAN
HAS GONE BEFORE

Therefore go and make disciples of all nations, baptizing them in the name of the Father and of the Son and of the Holy Spirit, and teaching them to obey everything I have commanded you. And surely I will be with you always, to the very end of the age.

Matthew 28:19–20

Summer is the time of year when many blockbuster movies are released. One night, my husband and I scheduled a movie date to see the movie *Star Trek*. Having grown up when the television series was in its prime, we couldn't resist this movie and were thoroughly entertained.

Dee Dee Wike

Star Trek conjures up great memories and some unforgettable quotations. When I want my son to do something, I challenge him to "Make it so, Number One." I pray that we all will "live long and prosper." The greatest challenge for me, however, is "to boldly go where no man has gone before."

Summer is not just a season for blockbuster movies. It is also the time of year that many spend their vacations traveling as missionaries to countries around the world. In summers past, several from our church have gone to places like Africa, South America, and China to spread the good news of salvation through Jesus Christ and help meet the needs of those less fortunate than us. In addition to all those whom God calls to short-term or full-time missionary work, there are countless more that he chooses to do his work here at home.

Are you bold enough to serve him and proclaim his salvation in the places where you work, live, and play? If not, pray for courage and his anointing and "Make it so, Number One."

HOW NOT
TO WORRY

Do not be anxious about anything, but in everything, by prayer and petition, with thanksgiving, present your requests to God. And the peace of God, which transcends all understanding, will guard your hearts and your minds in Christ Jesus.

Philippians 4:6–7

"It's my money, and I need it now!" is the slogan for a company that processes structured settlements. Thinking that we are incapable of assessing our own financial need in a challenging economy, advertisers are quick to remind us that we need, and perhaps are even entitled to, more money. They create a longing for things that are temporal and unsatisfying, when what we truly need is a heart of gratitude and a spirit of contentment for the things we do have.

Dee Dee Wike

Money is tight for most of us, and we worry about how we are going to pay our bills, buy our children's clothes and back-to-school supplies, and still have money left over to save for life's emergencies. I wish I had an abundance of money and never had to think about what I spend, but I don't. Still, I know that God will supply all I need as I continue to make knowing and serving him my first priority.

Whenever you start to worry about money, try thanking God for the simple things: hot water in your shower, air conditioning on a hot summer day, food in your refrigerator, and clothes in your closet. Most of us don't need the biggest and best of anything, except God. He is more than enough. He satisfies our longings, promises to be with us always, and provides everything we truly need to live day by day. Although sometimes we cannot see his hand of provision and don't understand his timing, at the end of every day we can thank him that our lights are still on, our children are well fed, and know that his hand of blessing has been upon us.

What are you worried about today? Rather than worry, try meditating on the promises of God's Word. While you are telling him what you need, be sure to thank him for all he has already given you. Pretty soon, you will find that his peace has replaced your fear and anxiety and that in him, you truly do have everything you need.

TOO HARDHEADED FOR OUR OWN GOOD

The way of a fool seems right to him, but a wise man listens to advice.

Proverbs 12:15

It's a wonder I have any hair on my head at the end of most days. Despite my best efforts and much prayer, being a mother sometimes has that effect on me. Truly, being a mom is the hardest job I have ever had, but in many ways, it is also the most rewarding.

My children are as different as two individuals can be, and I love them both for who they are. Both are extremely intelligent and very loving. My daughter is laid-back like her dad, content to build doll furniture out of Jenga blocks while watching TV or listening to music. Always eager to please, she will do anything—wash dishes, fold laundry, give me foot massages—to make my life a little easier. If I suggest something to her, she is quick to trust that I know what I am talking about and will usually comply without questioning what I say.

My son, on the other hand, is strong-willed like me. He has his own way of doing things, quite often not the way I would choose. He is passionate about the things he loves, especially music and his friends. He would rather hang out at the park than do just about anything else. Free-spirited, he has a mind of his own and is seldom on my wavelength. If I suggest to him that certain behaviors will lead to certain consequences, he will do everything in his power—in other words, do what he wants rather than what I ask—to prove me right. Unfortunately, that causes me a great deal of frustration and results in unnecessarily hard lessons for him.

In many ways, we are all a little too hardheaded for our own good. We have a loving heavenly Father who clearly teaches us the way we should go, but we all too often think that we know better. God's Word was written for our good, not to restrict us or make our lives a legalistic nightmare. His principles are as true and relevant today as the day they were originally written. The problem with us is that we fail to put our trust in him and in his promises. Instead, we live in rebellion and conflict with God, learning our lessons the hard way.

Do you think will we ever learn that Father truly does know best? The next time you have an opportunity to choose obedience to God over doing things your own way, try it God's way. You might just be surprised by the joy that results from doing his will instead of your own.

PRACTICE MAKES PERFECT

And now these three remain: faith, hope and love.
But the greatest of these is love."

1 Corinthians 13:13

Those of us who grew up taking piano or dance lessons are familiar with the saying, "Practice makes perfect." In reality, though, it isn't enough just to practice—we must practice perfectly if we are to perform perfectly, and even then, there are no guaranties that our performance will be flawless. We must be disciplined, committed, and willing to put forth the effort required in order to do our best, whether we are playing an instrument, competing athletically, or striving to maintain healthy and loving relationships with those around us.

In his Sermon on the Mount, Jesus said, "Be perfect, therefore, as your heavenly Father is perfect" (Matthew 5:48). In the context of this passage, Jesus was talking about being perfect in the way we love one another. Regardless of whether or not we *think* it is possible to love someone else perfectly, it is God's intention for us to strive for perfection in our relationships with others. The apostle Paul, writing to the Corinthians, said, "Our prayer is for your perfection. Aim for perfection, listen to my appeal, be of one mind, live in peace. And the God of love and peace will be with you" (2 Corinthians 13:9, 11).

Perhaps one of the most challenging aspects of life is getting along with difficult people. We all have at least one or two folks who irritate, annoy, or hurt us from time to time. How can we aim for perfection in our love toward those who wound us when we'd rather shoot a flaming arrow into their cold, callous hearts? The truth is we can't without God's help.

If we are to achieve perfection in our relationships, then our love must be patient and kind. It must not envy, boast, or be prideful. Perfect love is not rude, self-seeking, easily angered, or prone to hold a grudge. It does not delight in evil but rejoices with the truth, always protecting, hoping, trusting, and persevering. Love never fails (1 Corinthians 13:4–8). I don't know about you, but my love fails more often than not to achieve the level of perfection God desires for his children.

Jesus lived among us as perfect love in human flesh. He set the example of loving others that we are to follow in our own relationships. If we are to love as he did, we

Dee Dee Wike

must allow him to occupy our hearts as Savior and reign in our lives as Lord. Only then can we tap into his power to love others as he loved us. Have you taken the first step by inviting him in as your Savior? If not, take a moment to do that now and let his love transform you.

.

LEARNING TO LET GO

Train a child in the way he should go, and when he
is old he will not turn from it.

Proverbs 22:6

One of the hardest lessons I have had to deal with lately
is learning to let go. Anyone who has raised or is trying
to raise a teenager can surely relate. Finding the balance
between being a loving parent who desires to instill godly
character in my children and giving them enough freedom to make and learn from their own mistakes is a difficult thing to do.

The thing I find most frustrating is convincing my
teenager that I have only his best interests at heart. I know
the temptations he faces day in and day out and the con-

Dee Dee Wike

sequences his choices may bring. It seems that no amount of counsel I provide is enough to discourage him from making unnecessary mistakes and suffering the consequences of his choices.

I realize that at some point we all have to begin the process of letting go of our teenagers so they can grow into the people God wants them to be. As difficult and scary as that is for most of us, it is an unavoidable aspect of parenting. As we prepare them to meet the challenges of their world with wisdom and integrity, are we at the same time preparing our hearts for the day we must cut the apron strings by looking to God for his grace, comfort, and wisdom? Do we really trust him to take care of our children and mature them as men and women of God?

Letting go is a difficult process. Doing our best as parents and trusting God to do the rest is hard. No doubt we will make mistakes, and so will our kids. But as we look back across the years of our lives and see the hand of God and the redeeming power of his grace, we can trust that his grace is sufficient to see our children through the reckless abandon of adolescence and young adulthood into the years of spiritual maturity and fruitful service that are ahead of them.

NOT IN MY VOCABULARY

All a man's ways seem innocent to him, but motives
are weighed by the LORD. Commit to the LORD
whatever you do, and your plans will succeed.

Proverbs 16:2–3

Failure is not a word in my vocabulary, nor is it in God's. It
is a word I hear often in my household, as my son accuses
me of thinking he is a failure. Although I have a hard time
convincing him otherwise, nothing could be further from
the truth.

I looked through my concordance and did a search
of the word *failure* at www.biblegateway.com. I could
find only one verse that used the actual word *failure*. In 1
Thessalonians 2:1, Paul writes: "You know, brothers, that

Dee Dee Wike

our visit to you was not a failure." Although we some-times fail to accomplish a certain objective or task, that does not mean that *we* are a failure. As long as we keep trying, learning from our mistakes and shortcomings, and pressing on in our efforts to achieve the great potential God has for us, we can be confident that God will never consider us a failure. We are all simply a work in progress.

A search of the word *success* at www.biblegateway.com yielded twenty-four matches, compared with the one reference I found for the word *failure*. Does that tell you anything? God desires that we succeed in life. Success comes when we yield ourselves to him, follow his commands, and live each day with his glory as our goal.

How would you define *success*? I think the writer of Ecclesiastes said it best: "I know that there is nothing better for men than to be happy and do good while they live. That every man may eat and drink, and find satisfaction in all his toil—this is the gift of God" (Ecclesiastes 3:12–13).

FRIED GREEN TOMATOES

Then God said, "I give you every seed-bearing plant on the face of the whole earth and every tree that has fruit with seed in it. They will be yours for food."

Genesis 1:29

My backyard has been undergoing a transformation of sorts for a couple of years. I have always enjoyed planting flowers and watching them grow through the spring and summer months and have been greatly satisfied when the occasional tomato plant or watermelon vine actually produced something edible. As I have gotten busier, wisdom has dictated that I replace the annuals I normally plant with perennials that will come back each year.

Last fall, I began the process of turning a large azalea bed into a backyard vegetable garden to help feed my family. Since the front of my house needed shrubbery and I needed a garden plot in the back, I spent an entire Saturday last fall transplanting established azaleas from the backyard to the beds in front of my house. I lost only one azalea in the process and enjoyed breathtaking beauty when they bloomed this spring.

Despite a late start, I was able to finish weeding and preparing my garden plot so I could plant new perennial, fruit, and vegetable plants. The harvest wasn't plentiful, but the sheer enjoyment of watching things grow was well worth the effort. We managed to gather a watermelon or two and make a meal out of some fried green tomatoes.

Sometimes our best-laid plans don't turn out the way we hope, and we have to settle for something less or different. As hard as failure and disappointment can be to accept, God can use them to teach us trust in him.

"Many are the plans in a man's heart, but it is the LORD's purpose that prevails" (Proverbs 19:21).

FAIR TO PARTLY CLOUDY

Rejoice in the Lord always. I will say it again: Rejoice!

Philippians 4:4

In the Midsouth where I live, the months of March, April, and May are characterized by a typical spring weather pattern: soggy with a chance of sunshine. In fact, one year it rained so much that I couldn't plant flowers until after Mother's Day weekend.

Being cooped up and unable to work in my garden because of the weather doesn't help my mood, especially after a long, cold winter. Neither do the stresses of everyday life. When people ask me how I am doing, my answer is often "fair to partly cloudy." Rarely do I respond that I am doing great, although I have many reasons to feel blessed.

Recently, my family dined at a local restaurant we had not visited in several months. On the way there, we talked about our favorite waitress and hoped that she would be on duty. Although we are but one of many families she has waited on through the years, she has a gift of making us feel so special, as though we are part of her family. She is one of those rare individuals who lights up a room with her smile.

As we walked through the door of the restaurant and looked across the dining room, we spotted her. She greeted us warmly with smiles and hugs as though we were beloved friends, not just patrons of the restaurant. One of the other waitresses greeted us the same way. Their joy was both contagious and refreshing.

I can remember bringing home a report card from grade school on which my teacher wrote, "Dee Dee has a sunny disposition." How many people would make that same observation of me today? Sadly, very few.

The responsibilities of adulthood have eclipsed the innocence of childhood for many of us, and we have forgotten how to smile or have fun. We live under clouds of stress, disillusionment, and hopelessness, forgetting that the sun shines every day, even though we may not be able to see it.

If ever our world needed a good dose of sunshine, it is now. Jesus calls us the light of the world and commands us to let our light shine before men that they may see our good deeds and praise our Father in heaven

(Matthew 5:16). God wants his glory to shine on our faces so that others will be drawn to Jesus, yet so many of us walk around under the clouds of adversity with a pained expression on our face.

What does your countenance say about you? Does it reflect a deep faith in a loving God and a heart of gratitude for all he has done for you? If not, begin thanking God for his blessings and allow his joy to fill your heart. Pretty soon, your smile will return and be a blessing to those around you.

WHEN FEAR IS
A GOOD THING

Blessed is the man who fears the LORD, who finds
great delight in his commands.

Psalm 112:1

What are you afraid of? My daughter is deathly afraid
of thunderstorms, yet I love severe weather as long as
it doesn't come too close to my house. Some people are
afraid of losing their jobs in a tough economy or that their
prodigal children will never find their way out of a sinful
lifestyle and back into a right relationship with God. Fear
is part of our daily existence, but it doesn't have to steal
our joy or defeat us. In fact, the right kind of fear can be
a very good thing.

There are basically two kinds of fear: fear of God, and fear of everything else. Most of us are all too familiar with the latter kind of fear. It manifests itself as worry, anxiety, and stress when things go wrong, or we are afraid they will. It is caused by vision that is focused on our circumstances and what our finite minds can understand rather than on God and the unseen work of his hands. This unhealthy fear is quite often an unwarranted fear as well because what we fear may ultimately never even occur. Yet we become convinced that the fear is real, and we allow it to steal our confidence and joy.

"The fear of the LORD is the beginning of knowledge," according to Proverbs 1:7. This fear is not a state of being afraid but rather an attitude of awe and reverence for the sovereign God who controls every aspect of our lives. When we fully understand who God is, that he will do what he has promised in his Word, and that he loves us like no other, we will experience lasting peace and joy. If we live in reverence of God, we will have no reason to be afraid of him.

"He will be the sure foundation for your times, a rich store of salvation and wisdom and knowledge; the fear of the LORD is the key to this treasure" (Isaiah 33:6).

WALKING BUDDIES

He makes me lie down in green pastures, he leads me beside quiet waters, he restores my soul. He guides me in paths of righteousness for his name's sake. Even though I walk through the valley of the shadow of death, I will fear no evil, for you are with me; your rod and your staff, they comfort me.

Psalm 23:2–4

The twenty-third psalm is one of the best-known passages in all of Scripture. Commonly read at funerals to comfort those who mourn the death of a loved one, it is an assurance of God's presence with us no matter where our journey takes us.

Sometimes God does lead us beside quiet waters in the peaceful seasons of our lives. But he is also with us when we are facing difficult challenges and suffering great loss. To the young widow who knows Christ, he is her unfailing, ever-present love and comforter. To the woman struggling in her marriage, he is her champion and counselor. To children whose parents have divorced, he is a loving, heavenly Father who can be trusted with their fears and heartaches. Those whose bodies are ravaged by cancer and chronic illness look to him for strength and healing. Those who have trouble making ends meet know him as a faithful provider.

Where are you on your journey today? God is everything you need—everything. Pray to him. Trust him. He knows what you need before you ask (Matthew 6:8), and his grace is sufficient for you for his power is made perfect in your weakness (2 Corinthians 12:9).

HURRY UP
AND WAIT

Be still before the LORD and wait patiently for him; do not fret when men succeed in their ways, when they carry out their wicked schemes.

Psalm 37:7

"Hurry up and wait" is becoming an all-too-familiar phrase in my vocabulary. I spend a lot of time waiting on people to give me what I need to complete the projects they ask me to do for them. If I am not waiting on people, then I am waiting on something to come in the mail. The more I need what I am waiting for, the longer it seems to take getting here, and that really frustrates me.

We all have those moments of waiting that try our patience. Do we ever consider how God must feel as he waits on us to repent of our sins, lay down our idols, and choose the abundant life that is promised to those who abide in Christ? God is more than patient with us, but he longs for us to get on with the business of choosing a life centered in him because he knows that is the key to our contentment, fulfillment, and security.

God wants us to wait patiently upon him as we seek answers to our prayers, respite from the storms and stresses of life, and true and lasting love. When we charge ahead of him, we run the risk of stepping outside his perfect will for our lives, and that can be a dangerous place to find ourselves.

What is it that you are impatiently waiting for today? Peace, financial security, the homecoming of a prodigal son or daughter? Continue to wait on God and trust that his timing is perfect.

Dee Dee Wike

CALORIES
AND WIND

The wind blows wherever it pleases. You hear its sound, but you cannot tell where it comes from or where it is going. So it is with everyone born of the Spirit.

John 3:8

After several hours of severe thunderstorms one spring afternoon, my husband and I sat outside enjoying the sunshine and fresh air that lingered after the storms rolled through. As a cold front made its presence known, we discussed the wind, one of God's most amazing creations. Although the wind was invisible to our eyes, we could see and feel its effects as it cooled our bodies and rustled the leaves in the trees across the street.

Since we happened to be eating pizza while we enjoyed the breeze, I remarked to my husband that calories are a lot like the wind. We cannot see them, but we know they are in the foods we eat because of the effect they have on our bodies. Just as too much wind can be destructive, so can too many calories. When we consume more than our bodies need, we subject ourselves to the harmful effects of obesity and poor health.

In Scripture, we find many references to wind. At times, it is described as a destructive force, capable of destroying everything in its path. At other times, God has used the wind to accomplish the miraculous, as he did when he parted the Red Sea in order to deliver the children of Israel from Egyptian bondage. In the third chapter of John, Jesus uses wind as a reference to the Spirit of God who indwells us when we are born again.

We cannot see the Holy Spirit of God, but we see evidence of him in the lives of those he inhabits. How else can one explain abiding peace in the midst of extreme stress or a heart that loves a person who has an abrasive personality? The mercy of a caregiver, the wisdom of a teacher, and the compassion of a generous giver are evidence of God's Spirit at work in his children. Some would say that those character traits are the marks of a "good" person. But the Bible tells us that "there is no one who does good, not even one" (Romans 3:12). We are told, on the other hand, that "the fruit of the Spirit is love, joy, peace, patience, kindness, goodness, faithfulness, gentleness, and self-control" (Galatians 5:22–23).

Dee Dee Wike

When people look at you, what do they see? A doubting person who "is like a wave of the sea, blown and tossed by the wind" (James 1:6), or an individual of faith who is "in step with the Spirit" (Galatians 5:25)? As God's child, pray that you may "become mature, attaining to the whole measure of the fullness of Christ" (Ephesians 4:13) and of his Spirit who dwells within you.

A HELPING HAND

Carry each other's burdens, and in this way you
will fulfill the law of Christ.

Galatians 6:2

Why is it that we are reluctant to open up to others and
share our deep needs with them? So often we carry burdens too heavy for our shoulders when there are others
who would gladly come alongside and help us on our
journey. We feel that no one could possibly understand
what we are going through or have the time or inclina-
tion to help us with our problems, but nothing could be
further from the truth.

As Christians, we are called to help one another and
carry each other's burdens. That doesn't mean that we go
around "fixing" each other—that is God's job—but we
are to minister to one another with our gifts, talents, and
experience. We are told in Philippians 2:4, "Each of you

should look not only to your own interests, but also to the interests of others." Sometimes God allows us to go through challenges of our own so we can reach out to others in similar circumstances (2 Corinthians 1:4).

Is there someone you know today who needs a helping hand? Someone whose burden is just a little too heavy for his shoulders? Then lend a helping hand and receive the blessing that comes from sharing the resources and experience that God has given you for such a time as this. Perhaps that person is you. Don't be afraid to ask for help. God knows your need and is ready with an answer, but he may want to use others to encourage and guide you in your search for the solution.

REFERENCES

1 Merriam-Webster Dictionary. http://www.merriam-webster.com/dictionary/codependency

2 Chambers, Oswald. My Utmost for His Highest. http://utmost.org/are-you-obsessed-by-something/

Dee Dee Wike

AFTERWORD

If you enjoyed *A Pleasing Aroma*, please consider picking up a copy of my first book, *Good to the Last Drop: Refreshing Inspiration for Homeschool Moms and Other Busy Women*. Written primarily for women, *Good to the Last Drop* contains short inspirational reflections on the challenges of raising a family, managing finances, handling stress, and navigating tricky relationships. Seasoned with hope, humor, and the truths of God's Word, it will encourage and inspire busy women from all walks of life.

For more information on my books and speaking ministry, please visit www.deedeewike.com. To schedule a book or speaking event, please e-mail deedeewike@bellsouth.net or write to us at:

Dee Dee Wike Ministries

PO Box 193

Collierville, TN 38027-0193